The Real Estate Investor's Guide
to CASH FLOW and
Equity Management

D1560937

Other Real Estate Investment Titles by Jack Cummings

The Real Estate Investor's Guide
to CASH FLOW and
Equity Management

Choose the Investing Strategy
to Maximize Your Goals

Jack Cummings

WILEY

John Wiley & Sons, Inc.

Published by John Wiley & Sons, Inc., Hoboken, New Jersey.
Published simultaneously in Canada.

For general information on our other products and services or for technical support, please contact our Customer Care Department within the United States at (800) 762-2974, outside the United States at (317) 572-3993 or fax (317) 572-4002.

Wiley also publishes its books in a variety of electronic formats. Some content that appears in print may not be available in electronic books. For more information about Wiley products, visit our web site at www.wiley.com.

Library of Congress Cataloging-in-Publication Data:

Cummings, Jack, 1940–
    The real estate investor's guide to cash flow and equity management : choose the investing strategy with the maximum benefits / Jack Cummings.
        p. cm.
    ISBN-13: 978-0-471-79133-1 (pbk.)
    ISBN-10: 0-471-79133-4 (pbk.)
    1. Real estate investment. I. Title.
    HD1382.5.C8545   2006
    332.63'24—dc22
                                                                    2006004847

Printed in the United States of America.

10 9 8 7 6 5 4 3 2 1

This book is dedicated to my mother, who married as a child and, when her two children were teenagers, went into the real estate business. When I joined the family brokerage business, we were a grand group of Cummingses, with my father, mother, sister, grandmother, and uncle mixed in with another group of unlikely suspects to be active in the real estate game. How we all got along, and were successful at the same time, is a tribute to my mother, Virginia Jones Cummings.

CONTENTS

CONTENTS

Contents

CONTENTS

Contents

CONTENTS

Contents

CONTENTS

Real estate consultant and author Jack Cummings is focused on the nitty-gritty of one of the most important of all real estate investment decisions. Which is most important, cash flow or equity buildup? In his latest book, *The Real Estate Investor's Guide to Cash Flow and Equity Management*, he tackles the pros and cons of each of these two benefits. Although they are sometimes in conflict with each other, he shows you the primary *and* hidden source of each, how to identify which you need most, and how to maximize your ultimate benefit to achieve your goals.

Why This Book?

In his easy-to-read style, Mr. Cummings shows you the magic of cash flow, as well as the long-term benefits of equity buildup. This book is filled with dozens of true insider techniques. By the time you have completed this book you will have the confidence to set your own goals to maximize your return from your real estate holdings.

Why Jack Cummings?

Mr. Cummings has over 35 years of experience as an investor, developer, and realtor. His chapters are filled with concise, easy-to-follow examples of tips as well as investment traps that await you in the real world of real estate investing. He begins by describing exactly how you can increase both cash flow and equity buildup.

Then he proceeds to carefully illustrate how you can find properties that will offer the best potential for each.

Each chapter is presented in what Mr. Cummings calls his building block method. The goal for each chapter is presented. Then special terms and concepts that are especially relevant to that chapter are discussed. Then the real insider stuff is unveiled as he shows you how to increase the bottom line and to maximize your goals.

He describes and illustrates his points with easy to comprehend examples from his own experiences. He begins with the Magic of Cash Flow and ends showing you how to blend cash flow and equity buildup to best suit your age, experience, and investment needs. Each investor, Mr. Cummings stresses, has a different need to be satisfied. Whether the need is to maximize cash flow or to quickly build up equity, Cummings shows you the paths to those goals, and how they differ for each investor. His goal is to give you the tools you need to ascertain which of these two elements is to be maximized, how to get the maximum benefit, and when, if ever, you should switch from one to the other.

Chapter 2 opens a new world for investors who believe the three most important words in real estate are "location, location, location." Cummings quickly dispels this myth with clear evidence that the old trilogy is outdated. He says "location" is just one of the three most important words. To discover the other two is worth the cost of the book.

Cummings borrows insider concepts from his many other real estate investing books, selecting those critical to cash flow and equity buildup, and then adds new concepts that fit modern real estate strategies. He illustrates the mystic math of equity buildup and shows the miracle of using other people's money to double dip your way to wealth in real estate, no matter whether you prioritize cash flow or equity buildup . . . as long as you follow his examples and experience.

Do you want to have the safeguard that will protect you if the value of your investment drops to half of what you paid for it? Can you still profit? Why not, Cummings has shown investors the secret of how you can do this with every income producing property you ever buy. He has done it himself, and he shows you how easy it is. In fact, after you see how it works, you are likely to hit yourself on your forehead and say, *Why didn't I see that myself?* You will profit from this concept.

No matter if you are just getting started in real estate, are getting ready to retire, or have already retired, you will discover how best to achieve your personal objectives through simple, positive-oriented interim goals with the property you will buy, or that you presently own. Investment strategies are changing, and many concepts that were valid 10 to 40 years ago are no longer safe. Too many people follow real estate news that is spread by Wall Street, or your evening television news, and believe what they hear and see. Cummings spells out in big bold letters that real estate is local, not national. What goes on in your hometown is not necessarily following the same trends at the same time as in other areas of your country or state, or even in the town ten miles down the road.

This book is an easy and fast read. It will deliver the most bang for your buck you'll get today. In fact, it could well be one of the most important books you will ever buy to help you avoid mistakes, or to move back to the right path for maximum profits. You will know whether you should maximize cash flow, or set up an investment strategy that will allow you to quickly build equity. This book has the answer.

The Real Estate Investor's Guide

to CASH FLOW and

Equity Management

CHAPTER 1

What Is Cash Flow and Where Does It Come From?

The goal of this chapter is:

To Introduce You to the Mechanics of Cash Flow

Cash flow, as it applies to real estate investments, is the cash that is available from rents that you have collected after you have paid all the necessary expenses of that investment. Now, having said that, there is a bit more to the equation than just paying mortgage payments, insurance, utility bills, and that sort of thing. By the time you get through with this book you will know everything you need to know about cash flow, where it comes from, and how you manipulate things to maximize its effect on your lifestyle. You will also discover that there is another side to that gold coin. It is called equity buildup. By the time you complete this book you will have a new prospective on both cash flow and equity buildup. Best of all, the many techniques that I present, and the tips on how and when to use them effectively, will help you overcome the traps that await you in the real estate investment game. However, let's stay focused on cash flow for the moment.

Because real estate is a complex investment, it is capable of producing a slew of different benefits and perks to its owner. There are many of them, and for most investors the most important are cash flow, equity buildup, inflation fighter, tax shelter, as well as the obvious: a place to call home. Some of these benefits have value that can be directly related to cash-in-your-pocket. So when we calculate the benefits that one might get from purchasing real estate, it is important that we take into consideration the total package of benefits that are available to any specific investor.

Let's step back for a moment and look at the various terms and concepts that will give you a better grasp on the complexity of cash flow as a part of a larger picture.

Terms and Concepts You Need to Know

Cash Flow
Cash Flow after Taxes
Depreciation and Its Effect on Cash Flow
Contract Rate versus Constant Rate
Leverage: Positive and Negative
Cap Rate
WYSINAWYN

Cash Flow

Cash Flow = Income – Necessary Deductions + Other Cash Equivalent Benefits.

This is simple enough. You collect rents, and you pay the bills. These bills include everything that is pertinent to that property. However, it is possible that some of the items that are on the list of paid bills will actually be benefits that you receive that you have used to pay for out of your pocket. Like what? Say the investment is a shopping center and the operating company—which is really you and family members—get a company car, full medical insurance, and frequent flyer miles for any employee that travels on behalf of the company. These things have a value don't they? Of course they do. So, even though they may also be appropriate business deductible bills paid by the management company, they should also end up on your own private benefits and perks list, which are a result of the investment.

Cash Flow after Taxes

We live in a world that has provided each of us with a partner in just about everything we do. This partner is the Internal Revenue Service. So far, the IRS takes a kind look at real estate investors and offers them special benefits not handed out to investors of other commodities or assets. These benefits are the different deductions that real estate investors can take from the gross revenue that comes from rent collected from income producing real estate. A real estate investor can deduct the expenses of operation as well as deduct a percentage of any capital invested in depreciable assets.

Interest and Depreciation Affect Cash Flow

A big benefit, which people in the United States take for granted, is the opportunity to deduct as an expense of the operation any interest paid on money borrowed against the property. It does not matter where the money is spent; interest on any mortgage of real estate can, at this writing, be deducted as an expense of that operation. The deduction of capital invested in depreciable assets is the big perk because of the return to the investor of capital already spent.

For example: Frank purchases a motel for $2,000,000, and the IRS rules allow him to classify that investment as follows: $300,000 as land, which is not a depreciable asset so there would be no annual deduction (business expense called depreciation) for the land; $700,000 as furniture, fixtures, and equipment (FF&E), for which the IRS will allow an annual deduction spread evenly over 5 years; the balance of the asset, worth $1,000,000, could then be categorized as structure and its value spread evenly over 27.5 years.

Example of Depreciation
Motel that cost Frank $2,000,000 to purchase

Component	Value	Depreciation	Period of Years	Amount per Year
Land	$ 300,000	No	N/A	N/A
FF&E	700,000	Yes	5	$140,000.00
Structure	1,000,000	Yes	27.5	$ 36,363.64
Annual depreciation allowed during each of the first 5 years				$112,727.27

The effect of depreciation is that the investor can reduce the otherwise taxable revenue from the property by the amount of the depreciation. If Frank had $250,000 income left at the end of the year, after all operating expenses and interest on the debt had been deducted, assuming the mortgage was interest only, were it not for the allowable $112,727.27 deduction Frank's taxable cash flow would be $250,000. According to the 2005 tax rates, if Frank was married and filed jointly with his wife and there was another $30,000 taxable income from other sources (out of which all other allowable deductions and adjustments had been made), he would pay tax according to the following scale.

Schedule Y-1 – Married and Filing Jointly (or qualifying Widow(er))

If your Taxable Income is over	But not over	The tax is	plus	Of the amount over
$ 0	$ 14,000	—	10%	$ 0
14,600	59,400	$ 1,460.00	+ 15%	14,600

What Is Cash Flow and Where Does It Come From?

59,400	119,950	8,180.00	+ 25%	59,400
119,950	182,800	23,317.50	+ 28%	119,950
182,800	326,450	40,915.50	+ 33%	182,800
326,450	no limit	88,320.00	+ 35%	326,450

Following the above scale is a short version of arriving at his income tax, and the amount of cash flow that can be attributed to his real estate investment:

Steps to Arrive at Frank's Taxable Income

Taxable income from other resources	$ 30,000.00
Real estate income after all deductions except depreciation	250,000.00
Total taxable income prior to the deduction of depreciation	$280,000.00
Less depreciation allowed for each of the first 5 years	112,727.27
Taxable income after depreciation is taken into account	$167,272.73

Actual Tax as per Schedule Y-1

Amount over $119,950	$47,322.73
Tax due on the first $119,950	23,317.50
Plus tax on the overage of $47,322.73 @ 28%	13,250.36
Total tax due with depreciation	$36,567.86

Cash Flow after Taxes and Depreciation

Total taxable income	$280,000.00
Tax due	36,567.86
Cash flow after taxes with depreciation	$243,432.14

What Would Frank's Tax Have Been without the Depreciation Deduction?

Taxable Income without benefit of depreciation deduction	$280,000.00

Tax According to Schedule Y-1

Amount over $182,800	$97,200.00
Tax due on the first $182,800	$40,915.50
Plus tax on the overage of $97,200 @ 33%	32,076.00
Total tax due without depreciation	$72,991.50

Cash Flow after Taxes

Total taxable income	$280,000.00
Tax due	72,991.00
Cash flow after taxes without depreciation	$207,009.00

Amount of Extra Cash Flow Thanks to Depreciation

Cash flow after tax with depreciation	$243,432.14
Cash flow after tax without depreciation	207,009.00
Extra cash flow due to depreciation (that year)	$ 36,423.14

This illustration should impress upon you the benefit that depreciation (tax shelter) gives you when it comes to the maximum cash flow determination. Keep in mind that there are other elements that also can qualify as a cash equivalent benefit. What if the motel had a restaurant and Frank and his whole family occasionally ate there (for free)? How about the car that Frank drives, which was his old car, but now it has the name of the motel painted on its side, and the motel picks up the monthly rental tab? These are elements that should count to Frank's total benefits.

Therefore, if real estate may give you some income that is sheltered from IRS taxation, this is an immediate bolster to your cash flow. This book is full of tried and true insider techniques that will help you maximize whichever benefit your real estate investment offers you.

Contract Rate versus Constant Rate

Contract Rate: The contract rate of any debt instrument is the interest rate that is charged. If the contract rate is 8 percent, then the interest rate to be calculated would be 8 percent for the term. In mortgages, the term is generally 12 months. Be sure, however that there is not some fine print that indicates that the contract rate is per every 6 months or even a shorter period. A credit card, for example might seem to have a very low rate, say, 2 percent, but be calculated every month, to an outstanding 24 percent.

Constant Rate: In mortgage terms, a "constant rate" is the percentage of the amount owed that takes into account a steady equal payment over a period of time (months) that includes both principal and interest. This percentage rate gives you the total annual cost of debt service in a percentage form that includes both principal and interest. In this introduction to Constant Rates, I give you the basics to find it, and how it is applied to Cash Flow analysis and calculations. Later on in the book I also provide you with many different uses that can take you to interesting results in mortgage discounts, balance owed at any given point in the term of the loan as a couple of examples what Constant Rates can do for you.

In essence, the Constant Rate is a short cut to arrive at the required debt service that will include both principal and interest in one single interest calculation. For example, if you borrowed $500,000 at 7 percent interest and the payback period of time was 360 months (30 years) the monthly constant payment of Principal and Interest (P&I) could be found by looking in the appendix at the table titled: Constant Mortgage Rates 12 Monthly Payments a Year. This table covers a wide range of interest rates charged.

How to Find Constant Rates: To get an idea of how to use the table look for the 7 percent interest column and go down to the 30-year schedule. You will see 7.98 percent. This means that the annual total of those 12 months will equal 7.98 percent of the amount owed at the beginning of the period, in this case 30 years or 360 months.

What Is the Constant Rate for This Mortgage? Using the Constant Mortgage Rates table in the appendix, you discover 7.98 percent is the constant rate for a mortgage of 7 percent interest repaid over 30 years.

What Is the Total Annual Payment? $500,000 × 7.98% = $39,900. This is the annual total of 12 monthly payments.

What Is the Actual Monthly Payment of P&I? To arrive at the monthly payment divide this amount by 12:

$39,900 ÷ 12 = $3,325, per month.

How Does the Constant Rate Change as Repayment of Principal Continues? Take the $500,000 mortgage with an annual constant of 7.98 percent with total annual debt service (of P&I) being $39,900. At the end of 10 years of such payments, there would have been a total of $399,000 of payments made. The loan would now have 20 years remaining. The annual payments remain the same, so we need to know how much principal is outstanding. Another way to state this is "What loan amount can be repaid at 7 percent interest with a total of $39,900 per year in 12 equal monthly installments of $3,325 over 20 years?"

Using the table look under the 7 percent column at the 20-year line. The answer you will find is 9.30 percent as the constant rate, please review the following calculations.

Find the Existing PV (Present Value) of the Mortgage That Remains

1. Mortgage amount × Constant Rate = Total of 12 monthly payments.
2. This gives us: PV (present value) × 9.30% = $39,900.

3. PV = $39,900 ÷ .0930 (9.304 percent in a mathematical notation).

4. PV = $429,032.25 as the mortgage amount outstanding.

Calculate the New Constant for the Remaining PV at the Fixed Payment

New constant rate as it applies to the PV of $429,062.77 is found by dividing that amount by the total annual payment: $39,900 or back to the 9.30 percent constant found in the table under 20 years at 7 percent interest (contract rate).

How To Find Mortgage Terms That Will Give You a Desired Constant Rate with Equal Monthly Payments of the Combination of P&I

1. Ascertain the constant rate you want. Say you need a constant rate that does not exceed 8.5 percent per year for a mortgage that is paid monthly.

2. Scan the Constant Mortgage Rates 12 Monthly Payments a Year table in the appendix and make note of any constant rates that are close to, but less than 8.5 percent. To do this start with the 8 percent column and slide down until you find a number of years that offer such a rate.

3. You will note the following: Under 8 percent at 35 years, the constant rate is 8.52 percent which would mean that you would need a mortgage of 35 years and one month to bring the constant rate lower. This would suggest therefore that an appropriate constant rate loan of 8.5 percent could be achieved by a 35 year and 1 month term (421 months) at 8 percent interest.

4. Look for other combinations: Here are two: (a) Under 7.5 percent at 28.5 years the Constant Rate is 8.50 percent so you would need at least one more month or a total of 343 months to bring in a loan at the desired constant rate. (b) Under 7 percent interest at the 25-year period of time your constant rate would be 8.48 percent.

5. If you are using a mortgage calculator, you have to trick the computer to give you answers to the question: If this payment is the constant rate I want, what is the interest and/or term of years that will do what I want? So, you first find the amount of the monthly payment you need. To do this you take the loan amount, say $500,000 and multiply it by the constant rate you need, which in this case is 8.5 percent and then divide that by 12 to get the actual payment.

1. $500,000 \times 8.5$ percent $= $42,500$
   (remember to move the decimal) will give you the total annual payment required. The next step will divide that into monthly installments.

2. $42,500 \div 12 = $3,541.66$

3. Your monthly payment is $3,541.66

4. Using your mortgage calculator, begin your calculation by putting in the $500,000 as present value (PV) as the loan amount.

5. Calculate the mortgage terms using several different combinations of "term of months" and interest rates using the $3,541.66 as the fixed payment. The results you get will be the many different combinations of term and interest rate that will give you the desired constant rate.

Leverage: Positive and Negative

Leverage plays a major role in maximizing cash flow. Leverage, either positive or negative, is caused in an investment when you do not invest 100 percent cash in the property. By borrowing money, you can—when the circumstances are right—greatly increase the investment return on the capital you invest.

For example, assume you find a property that has a cash return of $120,000 after all expenses have been paid. You now purchase that property for $1,500,000, spending your own saved cash to do it. You have invested $1,500,000, and you earn $120,000. The earnings are at this point before income taxes, and the $120,000 is your net operating income from the property. It is also an 8 percent return on your invested cash. In this instant, you have zero leverage because you have not taken advantage of including leverage into the transaction.

Positive leverage is the boost in the earning potential of your invested cash whenever you are able to invest using other people's money at a cost to you that is less than the benefit you get.

Let's look at another example. To put this into simple terms, if you can purchase a $1,000,000 property that will provide $25,000 of cash flow before taxes and after all expenses including payment of a mortgage and invest only $250,000 as a down payment and borrow the balance due of $750,000 at a lower cost than the return to you from the investment. To see how this works, let's start with an investment return and a cost of money that are both the same rate.

Mortgaged Investment with Zero Leverage

Total investment:	$1,000,000
Down payment:	$ 250,000
Cash flow anticipated:	$ 20,000, which represents 8 percent return on the invested capital.
Borrowed Funds:	$ 750,000 borrowed with principal and interest being $60,000 per year.

If, for example, the loan was at 6 percent interest for 23 years 1 month, the annual payment of principal and interest would be approximately 8 percent of the total loan per year for the term of the loan.

This method of mortgage calculation combines both principal and interest to the debt service. Make a mental note right now that technically the principal portion of the debt service is not a "tax deduction" that you take when calculating your taxable income.

But cash flow is after all, what you have left, so it is more prudent to think in the way of total debt service when it comes to your spendable cash flow at the end of the year.

The above situation could easily fit many different transactions. Because cash flow is the cash left over (either before or after income tax has been calculated), it is important to remember this because mortgages often include principal payments. For this reason I will calculate cash flow in its pure state: what you have left at the end of the day after taxes.

Using the Constant Mortgage Rates Table for Constant Rate Calculations: Because quick calculations of this require you to think in the terms of "constant rate," look in the appendix for constant rates for 12 monthly mortgages under the 6 percent interest column and at the 23-year period. You will see 8.03 percent as the constant rate. Add one more month to the term and this will bring the payment down to the 8 percent Constant desired. You could find other combinations of course by looking for 8 percent constant rates under different combinations of interest and period of repayment. Here are two such combinations you will find: (a) 5.5 percent interest at 21.5 years is a constant rate of 7.94 percent and (b) 6% interest at 23.5 years is a constant rate of 7.95 percent.

Cash Flow with Principal and Interest Debt Service

Assuming the following calculations of income and expenses are correct, your cash flow analysis with *zero* leverage would be as follows:

Gross rents	$180,000.00
Total operating expenses	100,000.00
Net operating income	$ 85,000.00
Less debt service at 8 percent total cost per year	$ 60,000.00 (8% × 750,000 = $60,000)
Cash flow before taxes (8% of invested cash)	$ 20,000.00

In this example, your return is based on the fact that the cash flow will equal 8 percent if there is no mortgage or if your total debt service also equals 8 percent of the amount borrowed.

Review the Above Example

I introduced you to a couple of new terms here. The most important of them is net operating income, generally shortened to NOI. This is an accounting term that is the basis for several calculations. It is found by taking all revenue produced by the investment and deducting only the operating expenses. The only expenses that are not taken into account at this point are debt service and depreciation. This is critical because when you review potential properties or talk to sellers or their agents, the term NOI is often batted around and may not actually be calculated as I have just illustrated. Often depreciation is deducted, and debt cost may include both interest and principal amounts that can distort things a bit. But the major function of NOI is to find the capitalization rate of the property. This is also shortened to simply the CAP rate.

Cap Rate

The cap rate is found by dividing the NOI of the property (at the time you purchase it) by the property value.

Cap Rate Calculation

Property Value: $1,000,000.00

NOI $ 80,000.00

$80,000 ÷ $1,000,000 = .08

Convert this to a percentage by moving the decimal point two places to the right. Cap Rate is 8 percent.

This means that if there is no debt, and you paid $1,000,000 of your own money to purchase the property, you would expect to earn a 8 percent cash flow before income tax and depreciation calculations.

Create Positive Leverage by Borrowing at a Rate Less Than the Cap Rate

Positive leverage would occur immediately if you borrowed a large percentage of the purchase price at any cost less than the cap rate, which is 8 percent in the example being used. See the following example that reflects a reduced cost to borrow the needed funds.

Investment Using Positive Leverage

Total investment:	$1,000,000
Down payment:	$ 250,000
Borrowed funds:	$ 750,000 at 6 percent interest only
Gross rents	$180,000.00
Total operating expenses	100,000.00
Net operating income	$ 80,000.00
Less debt service at 6% interest only	$ 45,000.00
Cash flow before taxes	$ 35,000.00
Cash flow return (before taxes)	14% (of invested capital)

In the example above with positive leverage, I show the mortgage as an interest-only mortgage. Because there is no principal payment made (only interest) this mortgage will allow the investor to generate a higher cash flow than a mortgage that has both interest and principal payments. As you can see, there has been a substantial increase in the cash flow of an increase from $20,000 for the year to $35,000. Keep in mind that there has been no principal payment made against the mortgage. In the earlier case where the mortgage paid out at $60,000 per year, there would have been a principal reduction that would have gone out of your pocket and into the lender's pocket. In that instance, the lender has recovered a part of the loan principal lent to you. But your payment still remains at $60,000 for the entire term of the loan. Of course, at the end of the next 24 years you would have paid off the loan. In the interest-only mortgage, there would be no principal reduction, and the amount owed would remain at the original property value during the entire term of the mortgage. As you will shortly see, this is just one example of what you can do in the manipulation of interest and/or principal to affect both equity build up and cash flow.

20-Year Comparison of Cash Flow Mortgages with and without Principal Payments

Cash flow with zero principal reduction on the debt: $35,000 × 24 years $840,000

Cash flow with principal reduction on the debt: $20,000 × 24 years   480,000

    Added cash you can reinvest as you go: $360,000

Turn Negative Leverage into a Positive Situation

Negative leverage is what happens when you have to borrow the funds needed to buy the property at a cost above the cap rate. While not desirable, negative leverage is not always a bad way to go. Why? Because it might be the only way to go if you don't have enough of your own cash to make the deal. Also, notice I said that positive leverage would occur immediately by borrowing at below the cap rate. What if you knew that if you spent a little cash on fix-up and new furniture and the like that you could jump the rent to $225,000 at an increased operating cost of only $110,000 you would suddenly have a NOI of $100,000 and not $70,000. If the cost to improve the property was

$50,000 and the only money available to you was at 8.5 percent interest, here is how this would look.

Example of an Investment with Initial Negative Leverage

Cap rate at purchase: 8%

Cash invested: $250,000

Negative leverage on debt: 8.5% loan rate (interest only) vs. 8% cap rate

Original price	$1,000,000	
Fix-up cost	50,000	
Total price	$1,050,000	(reflects fix-up cost)
Less your down payment	250,000	
Required mortgage to close	$ 800,000	(at 8.5 percent interest only)
New or estimated gross rent	$ 225,000	
Estimated operating cost	110,000	
NOI	$ 115,000	
Less debt service at 8.5%	$ 68,000	
Cash flow before taxes	$ 47,000	

Even though this investment began with a negative leverage, it quickly turned to a positive situation as the income was increased. Later in this book, we will look at the many ways that income can be increased and deductions against that resulting income can be reduced. The effect of this double whammy is to greatly increase cash flow, or, if you would rather, use the cash to pay off all your debt on a faster pace. These facts are so important that your success in making truly worthwhile investments will depend on your ability to turn a modest investment into a windfall by increasing the cash flow or paying off debt.

An increased cash flow will quickly reflect a higher price that another investor will pay you for that property. In the instance above, if you had increased the cash flow from $25,000 to $40,000 and the investor's desired cash flow yield (before taxes) was an honest 6 percent, the $40,000 would relate to a down payment of $666,666.67 to the assumption of your mortgage of $800,000 or a total new value on this property of $1,466,667.67. Not bad as that is an increase of $416,667.67 in what might be a very short time.

WYSINAWYN
(What You See Is Not Always What You Need)

Remember your first typing class. WYSIWYG, which stood for "what you see is what you get," applied to most word-processing programs too, but in the world of investing and in particular investing in real estate, the key to maximizing either cash flow or equity buildup is to look well beyond what you actually see. I will discuss many reasons for this as you move forward in this book, but let me give you just a couple of the more critical aspects of this concept.

Minor Factors Govern
the Potential Return of All Real Estate

Zoning Ordinances: Zoning is the current law of any specific property that directs what, without a change in the law or rules, can be constructed on a specific site. These laws are called zoning ordinances and they may be in a constant review and frequent changes. They provide a prospective property buyer with a guide to the different types of use that may be approved on any given tract of land or lot. Pay close attention to the words "may be" approved. It might be that there are other circumstances of other laws that could also be applied in any given case that would reduce or expand the list of uses that may be approved. Okay, so you drive down a street and see a beat-up old home that looks like it is going to fall down. What are you actually looking at? Unless you know the zoning and all the other elements that go into the actual "what can you put there?" scenario, you don't really know what you might have found. A single-family home that is ready to be torn down, might yield a bonanza in the form of a fast food site, or a gas station location, or a high-rise office building.

Building Rules and Regulations: These are the vast lists of things that go into the actual construction of a building, and depending on the use it will be put to, the rules may vary. Other things can vary too, such as required parking; dry area water retention to prevent overburdening the city storm sewer situation; residential maximums for given areas of the town, county, or state to prevent overtaxing general services to those who already live in the area, and so on. Far more than that pretty lot that you see.

Economic Conversion: This is a subject very close to my heart, and one that you and I will dive into on several interesting occasions. At this point, let me say that this is the single most important issue about the bigger picture in real estate, or for that matter, the smaller picture. The key to maximum return on your investment may not be to build the most, or the tallest, building on the site. Which would you think would return the greatest economic benefit: A 400-unit condominium apartment building in a super-hot market? Or a 200-unit condominium apartment building in that same market?

Hidden Limitations to Use: The answer to the above question cannot be ascertained without knowing what other limitations or restrictions might apply, and unfortunately, there can be many that are not apparent without a lot of research. For example, some building codes limit development to a maximum total square footage of building space. This is often called FAR (floor area ratio) and is calculated based on the total square footage of the parcel of land. A 4 FAR would likely mean that a developer could construct a building with four times the total square footage of the lot. But wait it isn't so simple (or logical). Not all parcel square footage is calculated the same, and not all FAR is equal because some times structured parking (a parking garage) is not counted in the total area. Other times, in others areas of town or with different zoning, parking is counted. Remember this if you think that what was the rule will always be the rule.

But consider this. If there was a maximum square footage of building that would be allowed, a new element now comes into play. How much per square foot can you get when you sell the condominium? If the answer were $650.00 per square foot, for any unit between 2,400 square feet and 4,800 square feet and the market for each size is more or less equal, then the answer to the questions is build as many 4,800 square foot apartments as you can. Why? Assume you would be allowed to build 960,000 square feet of building. That could be 400 of the 2,400 (say 3 bedroom 3.5 bath apartments), or 200 (4 bedroom, plus den and formal dining room, 4 bath apartments). But the larger units save 200 kitchens, many less bathrooms, and as many as 400 parking spaces (by Florida building codes). So the answer is clearly go with less instead of more when the gross sales support that decision.

But there are many other rules and regulations that lay hidden in city ordinances and building rules. Perhaps the beverage license law says you cannot establish a bar or lounge (that sells alcoholic beverages) within 1000 feet of a day care center. This might not be a problem, but if you purchased a site to construct a mega-nightclub and checked the zoning and found it allowed what you want to do, but did not drive around the neighborhood to see the day care center a block and a half away, you could be up against a major road block. Guess who may have to pay through the nose to purchase and remove the day care center?

In the end analysis, the sudden wealth that can come (sometimes as a surprise) from real estate investing is generally a result of all the development potential factors coming together to the investor's benefit. The zoning allows a million square feet of retail or office space, parking codes are half what they are everywhere else and parking does not count against the million square feet of space, and the city has just rezoned everything within five miles around this site as high-rise residential condos and rental apartments. What a find.

Getting to the Cash

Cash flow is a result, as you have discovered, of owning a rental property that produces more revenue than it will cost you to hold it, service it, repair it, and manage it. It is entirely possible that if you purchase a property that may not have such sufficient income, in which case you lose money. Income properties that lose money, or real estate that does not generate income (a vacant lot, for example), are called alligators. The antithesis of an alligator is a cash cow. I don't think further explanation about those two animals is necessary. What is necessary is to review the sources of cash flow.

Sources of Cash Flow

Existing rent

New rental opportunities

Increased rent potential

Reduced operating expenses

Cost of living and other increases

Restructured debt

Reduce or remove unproductive expenses

Barter for some needed maintenance

Cut out some maintenance expenses completely

Offer pay-as-they-play amenities

Collect on tenant violations

Let's review each of these so that you become acquainted with the assimilation of facts necessary to properly recognize when any of these factors may represent a potential in a property you are considering as an investment. At the same time, I will point out some of the hazards that may be present in what you see, or are told.

Existing Rent

Every existing rental property has one or more leases in effect. They may be written, verbal, a combination of a written document and verbal changes. The lease may have expired, be considered to be a month-by-month, by local statues, or be a present or pending legal action festering between the tenant and the landlord. Every lease should be carefully read, and you should never assume that every document you are handed in a folder that says "form leases" is in fact an exact copy of each other. Forms that are printed out by a computer are easily changed to fit the needs of the tenant or the landlord at the time a new lease is executed. Rules from some tenants may not show up in leases for others, and so on. None of this should surprise you, however, and the older the building and the longer tenants have lived there the more likely to be such differences. This is a potential management problem that you need to understand and to recognize. But since we are talking about cash flow, it is very important for you to know the status of that tenant. Some critical elements to double check are:

Things to Double-Check When Doing an Audit of Leases

Start and termination date

Options to renew

How future rents are calculated for rollover or renewals

Penalty for late rent payments or other violations

Are there present outstanding violations?

What has the lessor promised that is different than other tenants?

Security deposit

The Estoppel Letter: Is there an estoppel letter (signed by the tenant and landlord that states that the answers to all of the above are correct, and that the copy of the lease attached is the sole document without any changes or amendments or addendums added later)?

When reviewing existing leases, recognize that most lease situations will have built-in increases in the rents or other payments made by the tenant to the landlord. It is not unusual for a tenant to balk at signing an estoppel letter that has been drafted by the landlord (or management company). Why? Because the tenant may attempt to take, or rightly take the position, that there have been modifications to the lease that have changed some of the wording. The original lease might have had a provision that allowed for an annual increase based on the Cost of Living "All Items Index" as published by the United States Department of Labor and Statistics, which can be found by searching "Cost of Living Index" on the Internet. Suddenly the tenant recalls that there was a note added to the lease that put a maximum increase to 3 percent per year, or an overall increase not to exceed 15 percent for the 20-year term of the lease. These increases can be an investor's only opportunity to turn a modest investment into a cash cow (truly great cash flow investment). To suddenly discover that there is controversy over the tenant's interpretation of what a lease says can be a blow to the anticipated increases.

On the other hand, many property owners do not apply these increases to future income that they will not participate in. Built-in increases can be one of the hidden gems that you can find when you do a full lease audit.

New Rental Opportunities

Economic Conversion to a New Use: Economic conversion is the change of use to a higher economic opportunity. This can be an overall change of use, or simply an upgrade to a higher-paying clientele of tenant. The overall change might even be to tear down the existing structure and build something else that better takes advantage of the location, its zoning, and the needs of the community. A more modest economic conversion is to take a property, say a motel that is well located to be used as a medical office complex, and to remodel it into that use. Always consider an upgrade as a potential way to higher revenue, but never overlook that the overall cost that includes improvements and annual operational expenses may overshadow the gains in monthly revenue.

Change of Tenant Demographics: As a community goes through a change in the nature of its demographics, you may see that there is a new opportunity to reach out to a different kind of tenant. A strip store that consists of 15 shops that cater to modest-income working class families may have been the right choice of tenant mix 18 years ago when the center was first constructed. However, the change in the residential and commercial nature of the neighborhood might now be better tailored to retired individuals with a greater disposal income for different kinds of services. Of course, there is a negative side to any change of tenant demographics, and it is imperative that you do not invest in an area that seems to be slipping away from better paying tenants unless the price paid will make sense.

The events that cause a downslide of a neighborhood do not occur overnight, although they may appear to. By this, I mean there might be an announcement that there is going to be a major development in the area that will require new roads to cut through a nice residential subdivision. The day that appears in the newspapers or on TV is the day that things begin to slide downward. But the fact is that this project was likely going through its political and bureaucratic process for five years or longer.

Never invest in any area unless you know what is under discussion or has recently been approved but has not begun to take shape.

But do remember that any change will likely produce a positive effect somewhere in the area. It may take some careful thought to ascertain which area, and how will there be a positive benefit, which you can take advantage of, but there will be something, somewhere—so keep your eyes open.

Additional Rental Square Footage: There are two aspects here. The first is that it may be relatively easy to add additional rental space to an existing income property. The re-modeled garage with the existing apartment upstairs might become two apartments, or the two extra bedrooms that are added to turn one-bedroom units into higher rental op-portunities. The second aspect is the fact that not all square footage rent is equal. For example, an old two-story five-bedroom home might be converted into three or four ac-tual rental units without adding any square footage. What might rent for $2,000 per month to a family needing five bedrooms, might bring $850 per month from each of five tenants, each of which occupies a nice one-bedroom apartment in a homelike set-ting. That more than doubles the income, and the overall cost to make the changes may be quickly recovered. The value of the property may double in its resale potential as well. Naturally, any changes, which you may think would be great, should be carefully thought out, and you must be sure that the local zoning for that specific location will al-low your anticipated remodeling.

Creation of "Out Parcel" Rentals: Sometimes it is possible to acquire a property that as a result of a change of use has "new" land areas available for rent. A good example of this is any property that, because of its present use, possesses a current parking area that is no longer needed and that can be put to to other use. A new car dealer or large used car lot may fit this example nicely, as would a restaurant or other heavy user of parking space.

Increased Rent Potential

It is possible to increase rents the day you close on the purchase of an investment property. This occurs because you were clever, and knew that the property you were buying was being rented below the market, or that with a few simple, inexpensive changes or improvements the property would warrant a higher rent. Naturally, this will depend on how well you have done your studies of the area, and how good is your knowledge of the rental market. But don't worry; these opportunities will exist in almost every rental market. Why? Many property owners who have owned their investments for a few years or longer become lazy in staying on top of what is going on in the area where they own property. They also may grow attached to many of the tenants and are often reluctant to raise rents as often as would be necessary to stay in tune with the increases that are going on around them. Or it could be they are just sick of dealing with property management and instead of turning the property over to a professional management company, they choose to bail out and take a cruise or something. Couple this natural tendency to eventually want to avoid the hassle of dealing with people, and it is not difficult to find situations that fit many of the potential methods to increase cash flow that I cover in this book.

Simple investigation of the events that surround the ownership of a property can tell you what is in store in the bright future of your investing opportunities, such as, the history of rents in the area and how that history relates to the stagnant rent of the properties' tenants. Have there been any increases over the past few years? If not, take a hard look at the reasons why.

It is entirely possible that the neighborhood is going through a downward transition and the landlord has had to hold rents at the former rates, even though leases may have called for increases. Or is it that the landlord just does not care. Yes, that happens too. Be sure you investigate rent trends for any area you are looking at for investments. It is a good idea to look back at least five years of rental history, even if that means you have to compare other properties to the newer one that you are looking at.

Reduced Operating Expenses

Better Management: Any hands-on investor is apt to provide better management to a real estate property than its former absentee or part-time investor. When there is "outside management" taking care of the property, it is necessary to know something about that management. Is it on-site? If not, then the hands-on investor should be able to provide as good, if not better, management at a lower cost. Better management does not mean, however, that lower cost is the goal. It is possible and even likely that the property needs to be upgraded to a higher-paying tenant. This suggests that some TLC is essential to show there is a new pride of ownership where the old owner has let things like common area maintenance slide downward. Management is important, however, and scattered throughout this book are examples and tips on how to deal with many of the management problems that you can face.

Reduce Fixed Charges: One of the best ways to get an instant increase in cash flow over what the previous owner was getting is in the structure of the debt service. Already, I have shown you the advantage of an interest-only mortgage. There are other elements that can come into play that are more creative than an interest-only debt. Following are several more ways to bring down the overall cost of debt service.

Five Creative Ways to Reduce Debt Service

1. An interest-only mortgage. This has been discussed already, and it is nice to know that there are lenders who are becoming competitive in offering this kind of mortgage to prospective investors.

2. A zero coupon mortgage. In this mortgage, no payment is actually paid. Both the contract rate and the principal repayment plan are not paid to the mortgagee, and the corresponding amount is added to principal. As with any of these mortgages, there can be virtually any repayment period, interest rate,

and method of payment. Zero coupon mortgages will ultimately require a balloon payment in all or in part at a future date.

3. A deficit interest mortgage. This is a little-used form of interest-only mortgage that uses a reduced interest rate with the difference added to principal owed. This uses a bit of the zero coupon format where no principal or interest is paid during all or part of the term of the mortgage. For example, the seller is asked to hold a deficit interest mortgage for $100,000. This mortgage may call for a contract rate of 6 percent but only 2 percent is actually paid. In the first year, this would mean that, $4,000 is added to the principal owed. This would mean that at the end of the first year there would be $104,000 outstanding principal owed. The second year another 2 percent is paid (of the $104,000) so that $2,080 of interest goes to the seller and 4 percent or $4,160 is added to principal. The third year starts of with $108,160 outstanding principal.

4. A land lease. When an interest-only mortgage is not available, it may be to the seller's advantage to hold a low-payment land lease as a part of the transaction. Because this kind of transaction does not trigger a sale and the tax consequences of a sale for the part of the property that is made up of the land (being leased), the seller may accept a lower return on that part of the transaction. Because every penny might count in the quest to maximize cash flow out of the investment, investors should review every potential to achieve that. While holding the land that is now leased to the buyer of the buildings may require the seller to subordinate his or her rights to existing or new financing, in the right situations the continued income may be appealing to the seller. The seller who is sick and tired of the management problems may get rid of those while at the same time keeping some monthly income.

5. An option to buy. A buyer who wants to have time to improve the value of a property in order to increase rents, or to flip the property at a much higher price, may enter into an option to buy the property instead of actually closing

on the sale now. The buyer puts up option money, which is paid to the seller, and the buyer begins to improve the property using the cash that might have otherwise gone to the seller as a down payment. The prospective new buyer wants to improve the property to the point that much higher rents will be possible. The higher rents in turn allow a lender to look at the property with a new value in mind, which passes on to a higher loan amount. In the end, this process can be highly effective to a buyer who can do some or all of the fix-up work. The seller is taking very little risk, assuming that all the legal work is done properly from his or her point of view.

Challenge Tax Assessments: Just because the County Tax Assessor has raised your taxes does not automatically mean that is what you have to pay. You can challenge the assessment and quite often have your taxes reduced. There are tax reduction services that will take on the challenge if you are intimidated or don't have the experience or time to do it yourself. They usually are paid only if they obtain a reduction. They are usually paid a percentage of what they save you.

Consolidate and/or Outsource Maintenance: If your property does not warrant a full-time maintenance staff, look around for property owners in a similar situation, and combine efforts. Several property owners in the same area can get together and negotiate sweetheart maintenance deals with separate companies that offer specific services. Pool, garden, elevator, roof, appliance repair and service, HVAC service and repair, and so on can be attractively and economically obtained. The key here is that all the property owners work together in this. While not all neighboring property owners will join your plan, it only takes a few for each of you to save money. However, when you are just starting out as a real estate investor you may want to do as much of the work that you can yourself.

Reduce Insurance Cost: Insurance companies can be competitive, and you may need to shop around. Of course, it might be possible for several property owners to pool their properties with the same company or agent, and bargain for better prices and service. Often it is not prudent to try to reduce your coverage to save money. That can backfire if you have a total loss and the company balks at paying because you underinsured the property. Make sure you have a good insurance agent who, at least, seems to know what you will need in the way of coverage and shops around for the best insurance package. Here is one thing to make sure you understand about your coverage: what does it *not* cover. Have your agent go over the total coverage with you and question what is not covered. Something like loss of income due to damage, or sign coverage, might simply need to be added to the policy at an often-small additional payment. Some agents may overlook that aspect and, will quote you a policy that is lacking important coverage.

Cost of Living and Other Increases

One of the essential ways to cover yourself against the rising cost to operate your investment properties is to make sure that variables over which you have little or no control and which are direct costs in the operation of the property are passed on to the tenant. There are various ways to do this. In shopping centers, office complexes, and other large rental properties, this is often accomplished by way of a common area maintenance fee (CAM). This fee is paid by the tenant and is a part of the lease, but is separate from the base rent. The lease should have a provision that states "rent" as determined by state statute, is a combination of the base rent amount plus CAM plus any penalty for non-payment, or assessment for any item or cost that is the lessee's responsibility. The lease should also indicate that failure to meet the CAM fee as assessed monthly or during different periods of the year will constitute a default in the rent.

CAM is made up of a varied list of "pass through items" Some common ones are shown below. Specific maintenance costs or expenses that are unusual for your area may also be included (like snow removal, de-icing expenses and the like). More often than not, you will find a property where the tenant pays a base rent and a CAM. However, it is likely that the CAM does not cover all the expenses that go with the property. Take this as a warning. The seller may tell you there is a CAM that covers all the expenses to carry, maintain, and manage the property. But the CAM may not actually do so.

However, CAM is definitely the way to go with leases. In fact, one of your first priorities will be to maneuver all new leases, or renewals of existing leases (where possible), to a position where there are two charges that the tenant pays: base rent and CAM. When you do this correctly, you will shift all the variables of property ownership to the tenant. This is the CAM, and it covers a bushel basket of things. I have provided a list of many, but not all that you may need to include in your properties' CAM.

Examples of Common "Pass Through" Items for CAM Charges

AC and heating repairs

Catastrophic repairs reserve

Common advertising

Common area lighting

Coverage for insurance deductibles

General maintenance

Insurance

Management

Parking lot maintenance

Planned increases

Property security services

Real estate and state sales tax

Reserve for replacements

Roof repairs

Rubbish, snow, and storm trash removal

Utilities

Every one of the items in the above list can increase in cost as you own a property. For property owners who do not have CAM charges, the only opportunity they have to offset those increases is to increase rents. This sounds good in theory, but the realities of raising rent is that the items that could fit into a CAM charge do not increase at the same rate. Taxes and insurance, for example, can climb at astronomic speeds while a normal cost of living rent increase, might be the lowest increase of them all. The idea for better economic management of your rental property is to back into the actual CAM that covers all the operational expenses of the property. Start with the maximum amount you can collect from the tenant for the space, without thought (at this point) of how much of that amount is actual rent and how much you need to go to operations. Be sure to include a portion for management, even if you manage the property yourself. That portion of the income that goes to your bank account can be treated as if it were income from another job, or you can calculate it as extra cash flow. Examine the following:

Assume you have a 10,000-square-foot commercial building presently rented at $12.00 per square foot per year.

	Totals	Amount per Square Foot per Year
Total collections from tenants	$120,000.00	$12.00
Total expenses for the year including management	48,000.00	4.80
Total revenue allocated to base rent	72,000.00	7.20
Total revenue allocated to CAM	$ 48,000.00	$ 4.80

It is easy to show a prospective tenant how the CAM is formulated. It is, after all, the total that is spent to keep up the property. It is money that is passed through to others who provide the insurance, collect taxes, paint and repair the building, and so on. All you do is collect that money and pay it out. The actual benefit you get, as owner of the property is the base rent. From a negotiation point of view, when you show the overall charges to the tenant, the rent looks far more reasonable.

So what do you do? Move all tenants to a CAM charge plus basic rent as soon as you can. You will sleep better.

Restructured Debt

Debt can be restructured in many different ways. Some of those ways have already been discussed. If the goal is to maximize cash flow, then the cost to carry debt should be brought to its minimum. Unless the goal is to end up with a debt-free property, or there is no other alternative than to have built-in principal amortization to the lender, there is no good argument for the need to pay any principal at all. When long-term low-interest financing is available that is interest only, it should be considered. The restructuring of debt is not a one-stop-shop kind of event. It generally starts at the time the property is purchased—or even before, in the case of an option-to-buy scenario with later financing when the option is exercised.

There will be limits to how creative you can be in most transactions. The seller's refusal to participate in this process by holding some debt or other cash flow enhancement technique will be the major obstacle to overcome. It has been my experience however, that a motivated seller is the best lender in any situation. Often the seller will refuse to cooperate simply because they don't understand how to benefit by doing just that. A major benefit might be to attain the primary goal by going along with your proposal (or with a few modifications). After all, they walk away with SOLD signs in the yard. Selling the property *was* after all their primary objective.

You need the ability to help the seller understand how a creative technique works. This will improve your deal making ability. Continue to learn how insiders work to bring sellers to the closing table.

Reduce or Remove Unproductive Expenses

As you fine-tune your management skills, you will begin to find that you are spending money on services or items that can either be reduced or removed from your operational expenses. Sometimes the reduction or outright removal of the expense will come after you spend money to upgrade your property to a more automated mode of operation.

Heavy security costs might be greatly reduced after installing a more modern surveillance system and increased lighting during the night. More modern phone systems, even Internet telephone systems, are very inexpensive and are getting better all the time. A tie-in between your security system and the Internet capability will actually allow every tenant, and anyone you give the passwords to, to go on line at the Internet, click to your special Web page, and see live broadcast of every surveillance camera in the system. That, by the way, can be a real tenant perk that can bring you tenants you never would have gotten otherwise.

Sometimes the expense cannot be reduced, but guess what? You may be able to include it into the CAM fee as new leases are drafted. Keep in mind, CAM is a pass-through, which is paid by the tenant over and above the base rent.

Barter for Some Needed Maintenance

Barter is a big part of many enterprises as a way to reduce or even eliminate cash outlay for some important, and expensive, operational costs. Advertising expenses, for example, may be reduced to half or more of what you are now spending, if you look for ways to obtain all or part of the actual out of pocket cost for your current advertising programs. Do you have mail out material? Do you have TV or radio spot advertisements? Do you advertise in magazines or newspapers? If so, can you directly or indirectly offer something other than cash to the sources for those needs?

If your real estate has rental space for one or more of the companies that provide the services I just mentioned, perhaps you could give them a great long-term lease. They pay off part of the rent through direct barter with you, and you get a long-term tenant that cuts down on your potential vacancy factor—which most landlords have, no matter how great things go.

There are barter specialists that can be found, either by their direct advertising, the Yellow Pages, or word of mouth. Contact one or more of them to see how their special knowledge can help you through barter.

Cut Out Some Maintenance Expenses Completely

What is your long-term objective with any specific real estate investment? If your plan is to purchase something and operate it for a short period of time while your new building's plans are approved and you need time to pre-sell your new commercial condo office space, then your management approach to maintain your property will shift into a "repair only what is necessary" mode. Plan to fix the broken elements instead of purchasing new replacements. An old roof can be made to work for a few years if that is all you need.

Keep in mind that there is a trade-off in reducing your maintenance of your real estate. Let things go too long, and you will lose tenants. But if your objective is to lose tenants (who have long leases that may prevent you from building your new commercial condo), then this kind of management may work. If you choose that direction, my recommendation is to do so only after you have visited with each tenant (separately), and have let them know that the building is likely going to be torn down in a few years (past the time of their lease), and that only minimal upkeep will be spent on the property until that time. Be nice, and let them know so that they won't be spending on tenant improvements, which they later sue to recover.

Offer Pay-as-They-Play Amenities

One major cost is the continued maintenance cost of a parking lot. Just think of those acres of asphalt that need to be resurfaced from time to time, and the painting of all those white lines, and bumper stops. Add lighting costs, security, and daily or weekly vacuuming of the area, and the expense runs into many thousands of dollars. Well, office complexes and other kinds of facilities charge for the right to park. Even some upscale shopping areas have valet parking that is available, at a cost, of course. These are forms of getting the patron to pay for the cost of the upkeep for all that space.

Hotels put extra charges on room service, safes in rooms, and collect handsomely if you eat a 75-cent packet of peanuts from the hotel mini-bar. All pay-as-you-play methods offer additional services (if you want to pay the price).

Collect on Tenant Violations

It is not unusual that during tenant audits you find that some tenants have violations to certain elements of their lease that have either not been paid, or for which the landlord has not even notified the tenant of the violation.

Failure to notify a tenant of a violation might be the landlord's way of being kind, but if the lease has rules that need to be followed, then failure to enforce those rules tends to lead to other tenants learning of this lax management policy and to more of the same from more tenants.

Of course, a strong approach to violations can produce some added revenue, but it can also produce other benefits to the new property owner. It can be the first step to upgrading the quality of the tenants.

Real Estate Investment Examples
Applied to Cash Flow Situations

Investment property number one   A Four-Unit Apartment Complex

Investment property number two   A Commercial Building

These two investment examples will be the basis for different investment techniques throughout the book to illustrate how different approaches to acquisition, financing, and management can allow the investor to reach different goals with the same property.

Investment Property Number One: A Four-Unit Apartment Complex

Property Offering: Asking price: $370,000

Property Information: Four units built in 1964. Zoned RMN 15, Lot size is 50' (on street and alley to rear) × 125' or 6,250 square feet. Consists of three one-bedroom one-bath units at 600 square feet each, and a two-bedroom one-bath unit of 1,100 square feet. There is a single laundry room with coin-operated washer and dryer.

    Current rents are $750 per month for the one-bedroom units, and $1,100 per month for the two-bedroom unit. Each lease has a cost of living index increase limited to a 2 percent annual increase. All four leases were renewed in the past 12 months for another four-year term, each with an option to renew for another four-year term.

Positives: Location is within walking distance of Fort Lauderdale's most in nightlife and boutique shopping street, in the downtown district, surrounded by urban rejuvenation to upscale town-homes and residential development, mostly for resale. Walk to new elementary school, doctors' offices, beautiful riverfront historic park, churches, great public transportation, employment centers, and one mile from the Atlantic Ocean beaches. The property is currently zoned for 15 units per acre of multi-family development. Current new development in the area is selling between $400.00 and $500.00 per square foot under air, plus an additional $250.00 for un-air-conditioned space (garage and storage area). Rental market is very strong, and historically this property has rarely had a vacancy due to waiting list of tenants. Current rents are a good 10 to 15 percent below the market.

Properties on either side are original and over 60 years old. Each sits on a lot of the same size. Property to the rear (across the alley) fronts on a major street dedicated to professional offices. Because there is no debt on the property, no mortgage penalty is due. In general, the property is well maintained and has had a new roof within the past four years. All new doors (front and rear) are new as of the past year, and the building was completely painted inside and out within the past year. Units have had some upgrades such as new a/c units (one-bedroom units each have two window units, and the two-bedroom unit has central air. Flooring in all units is upgraded to either Italian ceramic tile or wood parquet.

Negatives: Leases have a lock on use due to their potential long terms. Owner has limited opportunity to increase revenue. Redevelopment use is limited to only two new units by calculation of current zoning and use allotted. There is no existing debt on the property, which can be assumed. Operating expenses, taxes, and insurance seem high, and may be going higher. Asking price based on current reported income would return approximately 7 percent on a 100 percent cash investment. It can be conservatively estimated that repairs and replacements could increase by $1,200 a year due to future replacement of kitchen appliances over the next five years.

Investment Property Number One Income and Expenses

Seller's Current Income and Expenses

Income Collected	*Annual*
(3) One-bedroom units at $750 per month	$27,000.00
(1) Two-bedroom unit at $1,100 per month	13,200.00
Laundry revenue from coin op. machines	864.00
A. Total annual income collections	$41,064.00
B. Expenses for the Year	
Accounting (year end tax report)	$ 250.00
Property insurance	2,300.00
Property tax	4,895.00
Water, sewer, electricity	2,510.00
Repairs and replacements	1,500.00
Building maintenance	1,800.00
Management	2,000.00
Misc. expenses	1,000.00
B. Total annual expenses	$16,255.00
Total net operating income (NOI) for the year:	$24,809.00

Potential Benefits to New Investors

These are benefits that either directly or indirectly benefit the current owner of the property. Future investors may also use these benefits, while at the same time creating other side benefits.

A Place to Live: My first real estate investment was exactly like property number one. My wife and I moved into one of the units and used the income from the other three to pay off the mortgage. Over the years, the mortgage was paid off, and as we moved from one home to another the income from one apartment has always more than paid my utility bill, and rent from the apartment we lived in has paid off mortgages on two homes. This is a form of shelter from inflation that doesn't stop giving.

Independence at Work: Many people buy real estate as a business that they and many of their family members manage. The ability to manage the real estate you own is a big bonus to you because it allows you to focus on the needs of the property. Hands-on operations force you to continue to upgrade both the property and the kind of tenants you will have to deal with. The business of management of real estate is not all that difficult either. However, it is wise to learn how to do things correctly from experienced people. Don't take the position of general manager until you have worked alongside people (you hire) who can help train you. Sometimes these people are the sellers who sold you the property.

Travel Deductions: If you are the owner of a property that is distant from your year-around home, you likely purchased it as a result of periodic visits to the area on holiday. Now, because these "holiday visits" are also devoted to the business of management of your real estate, you will benefit from the "travel expenses" that can be paid and deducted by the real estate business. A $2,000 expense, for example, that you used to pay for out of your own pocket, is now a business deduction from the revenue from the business. If your top tax bracket is 35 percent the shift of the $2,000 from a nondeductible expense to one that can be deducted saves you $700. Or actually puts an additional $700 back into your pocket. This is added cash flow.

Tax Shelter: Each new owner would start depreciation anew. As a rental investment, the value would be split between the "land only" and all the improvements on the land.

A good estimate of such a split for this investment would be 25 percent of the cost to purchase as land and the balance spread between improvements and personal property (FF&E). Since the current owner has owned the property for 30 years, the structure has been fully depreciated, and only replaced FF&E is available for depreciation. Current depreciation is $1,200.00 per year.

Management: The $2,000 management fee might go directly into the owner's pocket. This is work, of course, but it is also added cash flow. The ability of several real estate investments to pay you for the time it takes for you to own and care for your property is a form of financial independence that you should not overlook. You are your own boss here, so never forget it. Consider forming a separate management company.

Investment Property Number Two: A Commercial Building

Property Offering: Asking price: $1,700,000

Property Information: Six commercial units built in 1964. Zoned CB-1 (limited commercial use). Each unit consists of 1,250 rental square feet of area, and each space has its own central a/c unit. Gross rental area is 7,500 square feet. The physical size of each unit is appx. 17′ x 75′.

Current base rents average $1,850.00 per month. There is an additional CAM charge of $293.00 per month, which covers taxes and insurance. Each lease has a cost of living index increase limited to a 4 percent annual increase. Five leases recently renewed (in the past 12 months) for another five-year term. The sixth unit is on a one-year lease, with option for an additional three years. Tenant also pays Florida Sales Tax (6 percent of base rent), which is over and above the base rent. Sales tax collections or payments to state are not shown in the Seller's Current Income and Expenses report to prospective buyers.

There is no existing financing, but the seller indicates a willingness to hold a new first mortgage equal to 75 percent of the asking price. Terms to be negotiated.

Positives: Excellent location on prime commercial boulevard. Near three major hospitals, several public and private schools, and in an upper-scale residential part of town. The building is a single story "store front" building with good signage and ease of access. There is a public alley at the rear of the building, allowing for additional parking and ease of delivery to the tenants. The building meets Americans with Disabilities Act (ADA) access to the front entry of each rental bay. There are new accordion storm shutters for each of the bay plate glass windows that allow for quick and easy protection from storms. The building has a good history of occupancy and is currently 100 percent occupied. The operating income and expenses provide management expense, and owner has indicated willingness to continue management of the building for up to five years from the date of closing if the buyer wishes. A new owner capable of self-management of the property may find ample room to improve the long-term cash flow of the property by reduction of operating costs and increasing the present revenue.

Negatives: There is approximately $8,000.00 in replacements of A/C units that will be needed within the next two years. The current roof (flat) is 5 years old, with 15 years remaining on its guarantee. The current zoning and building codes would require more parking than this building provides, but despite that fact, the building has not suffered loss of tenants due to its prime location. Existing leases do not provide owner with a full CAM pass through, so rising operating costs may reduce the yield to a new owner.

Property Number Two Income and Expenses

Seller's Current Income and Expenses

(A)	Income and CAM collected	*Annual*
	(6) Commercial units at $1,850 per month	$133,200.00
	(6) CAM collections at $293 per month	21,096.00
(A.)	Total annual income & CAM collections	$154,296.00
(B)	Expenses for the year	
	Accounting (year end tax report)	$ 750.00
	Advertising budget	1,500.00
	Property insurance	6,200.00*
	Property tax	14,896.00*
	Water, sewer, electricity charges	3,750.00
	Repairs and replacements	5,500.00
	Building maintenance	3,800.00
	Management expenses	7,500.00
	Misc. expenses	3,500.00
B.	Total Annual Expenses	$ 40,721.00
	Total Net Operating Income (NOI) for the Year:	$ 113,575.00
	CAP Rate (NOI divided by Price)	
	$113,575.00 ÷ $1,700,000 = 6.68 percent	

Not shown above is the seller's depreciation, see the following for Added Benefits.

---

*The two items that are collected by CAM.

Added Benefits Available to New Owners

Tax Shelter: The present owner acquired this property one year ago. The current depreciation was based on a purchase price of $1,250,000 and is divided as follows:

Depreciation Schedule for Property Number Two

Category	Value	Years to Depreciate	Annual Depreciation
Land:	$250,000	0	
FF&E	30,000	7	$ 4,285.71
Structure	970,000	39	24,871.79
Total Annual Depreciation			$29,157.50*

Mortgage Interest Payments: Assume that you purchased this property at its full asking price of $1,700,000 putting $350,000 down, since you were able to negotiate a really good purchase mortgage in the amount of $1,350,000 at an interest charge of 7 percent that required you to pay 5 percent per year of interest on the principal outstanding and the balance of 2 percent would be added to principal over six years.

To simplify this example, assume that there is one interest payment due at the end of each year. At the end of six years the mortgage would balloon (become due and payable) and you would either sell the property at that time, pay off the loan from cash you have saved up, or refinance the loan. Look at the dynamics of this kind of mortgage.

---

*This depreciation schedule may or may not be the best one for you and is used here only to illustrate what can occur. Depreciation can be a complicated process to establish, since the date on which the property was acquired can affect the schedule used. Always follow the advice of your accountant, but make sure that your accountant understands your long-range goals. If maximum cash flow is your objective, then confide to your accountant that fact.

Principal Owed at the Start of the Mortgage Payment Schedule: $1,350,000.

7% interest: 5% paid and 2% added to Principal Owed with Balloon at end of six years

A	B	C	D	E
	Principal at	*Interest Paid*	*2% of B Added*	*New*
	the start of	*5% of*	*to Principal*	*Principal*
Year End	*the year*	*B*	*B*	*Owed*
1	$1,350,000	$67,500	$27,000	$1,377,000.
2	1,377,000	68,850	27,540	1,404,540.
3	1,404,540	70,227	28,090.80	1,432,631
4	1,432,631	71,631	28,652	1,461,283
5	1,461,283	73,064	29,225	1,490,508
6	1,490,508	74,525	29,810	1,520,318
Total interest paid				$ 425,797
Total unpaid interest and principal due at the end of six years				$1,520,318

Review This Mortgage: The interest rate, also called the contract rate, is 7 percent; however, only 5 percent is actually paid and the remainder (2 percent) is added to the principal owed. There are benefits to this kind of schedule for both the buyer and the mortgage holder. First of all, it could be that the best alternative the buyer could get was an amortized mortgage with a constant rate (of interest and principal combined) of 7.85 percent. That mortgage would have an annual debt service of $105,975, which would reduce the cash flow before taxes by $38,475.00. Secondly, as the plan for this investment is to improve the cash flow and sell it on or before the balloon payment of the mortgage, the shift of the 2 percent interest each year to the principal owed maximizes the cash flow for the buyer, and allows the mortgage holder to get an additional one-quarter percent of interest.

Over the six years of anticipated ownership it would be likely that the revenue from this property would increase, which would, in turn, cause the value of the property to also increase. If the property went up in value 5 percent per year by the end of the six years the property would be worth: $2,278,162.50, which is an increase of $578,162.50 over the original purchase at $1,700,000. Apply both the mortgage and the depreciation shown in this example to the income and expenses statement illustrated below:

Revised Income and Expense Calculations for Property Number Two

Mortgage interest for the first year	$ 67,500.00	
Depreciation calculated previously	$ 29,157.50	
(A.) Total annual Income & CAM collections		$154,296.00
(B) Expenses for the year		
Accounting (year end tax report)		$ 750.00
Advertising budget		1,500.00
Property insurance		6,200.00*
Property tax		14,896.00*
Water, sewer, electricity		3,750.00
Repairs and replacements		5,500.00
Building maintenance		3,800.00
Management expenses		7,500.00
Misc. expenses		3,500.00
B. Total annual expenses		$ 40,721.00
Total Net Operating Income (NOI) for the Year:		$113,575.00
Debt Interest the first year	$67,500.00	
Depreciation taken	$ 29,157.50	

_____

*The two items that are collected by CAM.

Total Deductions from NOI to arrive at Taxable Income		96,657.50
Taxable Income from This Real Estate Investment		$ 16,917.50
Assume income is taxed at 25 percent (see Schedule on page 4)		× 25%
Actual Tax Due		$ 4,429.37
Real Cash Flow Benefits		
NOI for the year		$113,575.00
Less		
Debt Interest paid	67,500.00	
Income Taxes on Income from the Investment	4,429.37	
		71,429.37
Cash flow after taxes		$ 42,145.63
Actual yield after taxes on invested $350,000		12.04%

This investment has been leveraged from the original cap rate of 6.68 percent to nearly double that amount. This has occurred solely due to the method of debt service and the reduction of income taxes through the use of the tax shelter.

Can you think of other things the new owner might have done to increase the cash or cash equivalent return? How about taking on some of the management duties? Or paying close attention to rental increases that may occur before the end of the year?

CHAPTER 2

What Is Equity Buildup and Where Does It Come From?

> The goal of this chapter is:
>
> **To Introduce You to the Benefits of Equity Buildup**

If you purchase a property for $1,000,000 and pay all cash, and the property appreciates in value over 10 years to be worth $2,000,000, you have an doubled your equity in this property. That is a good return. However, you can introduce leverage into this equation, purchase the property with $200,000 down, and get the seller to hold a first mortgage for the balance of $800,000. Make things even better, and let the income from rents that the property generates pay off that mortgage over that same 10-year period. You now have a property worth $2,000,000, and you have increased your equity from $200,000 to $2,000,000. Things are getting better now.

However, carry this one step more. Why not improve the rental income as you go so that after the second year you start generating cash flow as well as paying off the mortgage. Now you have an investment that is producing a spendable return as well as being on its way to being free and clear.

Free and clear ownership of income producing real estate is a goal that many people want to attain. There are many reasons for this, and yet, it comes at a trade off to giving up cash flow. Nonetheless free and clear ownership is far less stressful than managing investments that are highly leveraged, and for many people the long-range goal of building equity is a good way to enter retirement.

This chapter will take you into the world of building equity quickly, with a positive approach to maximizing the economic capability of the investment.

Review each of these concepts.

Terms and Concepts You Need to Know

The Three Most Important Words of Real Estate Are Not "Location, Location, Location"

Double Dip to Big Returns

The Six Elements of Value in Real Estate

The Three Most Important Words of Real Estate Are Not "Location, Location, Location"

They are: "Location, Use, and Approval." This point is so important I find that in almost every book I write I include a section on this topic. If you have read other books I have written, do not just skip over this part, there is more to it each time I discuss it.

Location: Every item of real estate has something unique about it. There are no two exact anything when it comes to real property, because each occupies a different location. Even the same model of condominium apartments in the same building has something unique from the one right next to it. However, in general terms, the idea of location is more a function of two other elements, which is difficult to separate from just the geographic location where a property is found. These two elements are "time" and "opportunity." You know how the saying goes: "He was there at the right place at the right time and went for it."

Timing is critical because real estate functions in cycles. In any given market area, values of different types of real estate are going up while others are going down. Different cities might be in opposite cycles for homes or office buildings, so you cannot simply look at a cycle in one part of the country and rush to another location hundreds of miles distant and cash in on what you are sure is going to happen. At any given location there will be a time when it is ripe to buy or to sell. If you miss out on that time, you will have to settle for an off peak or bottom time, and wait out the cycle. Now there is one exception to this, and I will discuss it later on in this chapter. Look for it; it is "economic conversion."

Opportunity is an event that you have to recognize. As you learn your market area, and develop what I call a comfort zone, you will begin to see the opportunities that have been right under your nose all the time. The key is to be able to act on that opportunity. It will not hang around waiting for you to buy or sell, because there are others willing to act.

Use: The second of your new three important words is *use*. Use is, after all, what the investor wanted the property for in the first place. The greatest location to build a bowling alley is not a viable choice for the investor who wants to own and operate a Burger King restaurant. A specific use is determined by zoning ordinances and can be restricted by other laws of the community, even when the zoning appears to allow a specific use. Zoning ordinances are important because if there were none, you would find that communities would be developed with an array of uses scattered about the city. Industrial areas might pop up next to residential homes, or junkyards across from schools. Uses evolve as a town grows and are subject to constant review and modification.

Every investor needs to be acquainted with the zoning ordinances and building codes, and what other laws there are that can modify, restrict, or even disallow a use. It is possible, however, for an investor to petition for a change in the zoning, and many investors make their millions by taking a property that is zoned for one use and obtain a new, more economically compatible zoning that allows a greater and/or more viable use.

Approval: The third word of this trilogy is *approval*. Some communities are so much against development that no matter what the zoning says, no matter how lax the building codes are, there are those in power that will find a way to stop just about anything they don't want to be built or operated in their community. "That's not fair," you might say, and I will agree with you. But it is a fact of life and works on the rule that "those who got there first, get to stop those who come later from doing what those who got their first already did." You get the picture I would suspect. Now, sometimes there are investors with really deep pockets who can, and do, hire expensive lawyers and land planners with better credentials than those on the city staffs. These investors are willing to go to court and fight the city. Sometimes these deep-pocketed people win. Sometimes they do not.

Therefore, an approval for a truly viable project is worth its weight in buckets of diamonds. That is, unless the right time has slipped past, and the opportunity for success has been lost.

Double-Dip to Big Returns

Income producing real estate is exciting because it functions on what I call "the double-dip" investment plan. It is simple to understand and very important to use. To start this plan, you have to understand that we are talking about using other people's money in the investment cycle. This begins with money from a lender. Lenders willing to give you money at a modest interest rate are very plentiful in the United States. This is not the case in many parts of the world and we in the United States tend to take this for granted. The long-term fixed modest rate mortgage that you can get from any savings and loan institution in the United States is unique to very few countries. Try getting a 30-year 6 percent loan in South America, or Africa, or Asia and you will understand what I mean.

Okay, you buy a property that costs $1,000,000, and you borrow 75 percent of the purchase price (or more if the lender likes both you and the project). That $750,000 mortgage must be paid back at whatever terms you can negotiate with the lender. Lenders today have many plans to fit your investment goals, so do not jump at the first one offered. Say you take a 30-year amortized loan repayment at 6 percent interest for the term of the mortgage. That would give you a repayment plan of $4,573 a month over the 360 months of the repayment schedule.

At that repayment schedule, you would have to make a payment to the lender every month, right? Wrong. You do not because you are going to double-dip and let your tenants make the payment for you. At the end of 10 years, you now owe $615,151 because your tenants have paid off part of the original loan. At the end of 30 years, you would owe nothing, and you got to that position without even reaching into your pocket (really that's how it works).

Your mortgage payment that the tenants pay never goes up. It will be (in this re-payment plan chosen) $4,573 a month for the life of the loan. However, what about your tenants rent? Does it remain the same for the life of your loan? No, and this is the beauty of the double-dip plan. Take a look at a tenant rent roll with annual increases to the rent as tied to the cost of living "all items" index. Let's assume that the index goes up 4 per-cent per year each year. Consider the annual debt service is $54,876. (12 × $4,573).

First Seven Years of a Tenant Rent Roll with a 4 Percent Annual Cost of Living Increase

Year	Tenants' Rent	Less Mortgage Payment	Net to Owner
1.	$400,000	$54,876	$345,124
2.	416,000	54,876	361,124
3.	432,640	54,876	377,764
4.	449,945	54,876	395,069
5.	467,942	54,876	413,066
6.	486,660	54,876	431,784
7.	506,126	54,876	451,250

What is happening above is the leases are going up, but the mortgage payment (which is deducted from this rent to give the investor his or her cash flow) does not increase. Because of this, the increases to the cash flow are at a greater percent every year. This is one of the double-dip benefits you can take advantage of.

The Six Elements of Value in Real Estate

Is the foundation of all wealth

Is necessary

Is expected to go up in value

Is full of perks

Pays for the increases in the cost of living

Instant value by design

Let's review each of these elements.

Is the Foundation of All Wealth

Real estate begins with the land—land that we farm, live on, mine under, and investigate for oil or minerals. People fight wars over land, and if you don't have any or can't afford to rent any, then the question of wealth is moot. Land and the space it occupies are, with very few exceptions, eternal. You can count on its existence for hundreds of generations. What is made of the land, however, can be changed, and the opportunity to start anew is one of the fundamental factors in the renewal of wealth.

Is Necessary

Land and the buildings on it are essential to economic development and civil structure as we know it. Sure, there are communities that live afloat in river deltas and on ice flows, but they hardly can be called thriving economic communities. The inability of such non-nomadic communities to simply get up and go, and the un-universality of real estate actually is one of the real benefits that real estate extends, and it also creates a stable commodity in the long run.

Is Expected to Go Up in Value

The value of real estate is affected by many things, and one of them is the simple perception that its value is expected to rise in between the time you purchased it and when you go to sell it. For some, the rise occurs almost overnight, for others not as quickly. The fact of the matter is that not all real estate does go up in value. This is especially true if you index real estate to the cost of living. Nonetheless, for the prudent real estate investor who knows what to look for, and avoids highly speculative and over-leveraged situations, real estate is a very safe long-term investment.

The unique magic about real estate is that you can profit very handsomely, even if you sell for half the price you paid for it. Sound like a Nigerian proposition? Consider the following real-life example. Robert purchased a vacant lot for $25,000 giving the seller $5,000 for a one-year option to purchase the lot. If he closed within nine months, though, he could count the full $5,000 he paid for the option as part of the purchase price.

During the nine months, Robert had plans drawn up to construct a six-unit apartment building, where he planned to live in one of the apartments and rent out the other five. By using the option technique, he was "buying" the nine months free of any real cost to him. As he got the full $5,000 as part of the purchase price, the option, as it turned out, was free.

By the time the nine months were up, Robert had a building permit in hand, a development loan committed to the project, and a general contractor lined up to break ground the day after the closing.

At the closing table he paid off the lot owner with the balance owed of $20,000, went to the bank, and closed on the development loan, and because his proforma for the units showed the land residual value of the lot at $75,000, he was able to finance the full development of the six units with the bank.

The year was 1970, and the 4,500-square-foot building (5 one-bedroom units of 650 square feet each, and 1 two-bedroom unit of 1,250 square feet), was $125,000. The $125,000 mortgage was at 6 percent amortized over 30 years. This gave Robert a monthly principal and interest (P&I) payment of $ 750.00 per month. This payment plus the basics of the investment, namely—real estate taxes, insurance, and general maintenance (which Robert expected to do himself)—could be covered from the rental of four of the apartments. That left Robert with some spending cash from the fifth apartment, and, of course, his own two-bedroom unit as his home.

Robert's actual investment is $25,000 to the mortgage. But, who paid off the mortgage over those 30 years? Not Robert. His tenants.

Over the 30 years, the mortgage was completely paid off. In addition to living free and paying off the mortgage, he took in over $100,000 in extra earnings. Now, here's the question? If he sold the property at the end of 30 years for anything over the total cost when he built the apartment would that be a great investment? That would be anything over $150,000 (mortgage of $125,000 plus $25,000 of his own cash). Well if he sold for half that amount, he would get $75,000 that is three times the cash he had invested. Although we know Robert could do much better than that, this proves the point that the value doesn't have to go up for the real estate investor to make money. The magic is "double-dipping with other people's money."

Remember, Robert used $25,000 of his own money. He got nine months of time without any additional cost and obtained all the approvals he needed, including a $125,000 new loan to construct the apartment building. Almost immediately, he was meeting his mortgage payments and the other costs of owning the apartment building. So, he starts with other people's money (the bank's money), and then pays that loan off with other people's money (the tenants). Over the 30 years of his ownership, the rents went up, but the mortgage payment did not. He was experiencing the best of all real estate investment worlds.

Is Full of Perks

Already I have mentioned a number of perks that come with real estate ownership. For many people, real estate provides them with a full family of employment opportunities. These business-oriented real estate investments range from restaurants, retail operations, hotels and motels, to a nearly endless list of large and small business operations that either own or rent their location and facilities. Just to remind you, when you own and operate a business, especially a family owned and operated one, there are solid business deductions for services you likely now have to reach into your own pocket to pay, and have to do so without getting a tax break at the same time. What kind of deductions? How about full medical coverage, combination business and holiday trips, company car, and so on.

I would recommend that you sit down with your accountant and discuss the different ways to do this. It might be that you establish either an S or a C corporation as the management company for your real estate. Go over which of these or other business formats would be best for you, then go for it. You will be glad you did.

Pays for the Increases in the Cost of Living

Rental properties, when even modestly maintained, will keep abreast of any cost of living increases. This is a great comfort to an investor who wants to build a retirement base.

Chuck retired from the army at 45 years of age and purchased a small 17-unit motel not far from the beach in Fort Lauderdale. The property cost him a total of $500,000 with $100,000 down, which he had saved, plus a small inheritance. He and his wife lived in a nice three-bedroom apartment behind the motel office, and operated the facility nine months a year. They had two employees that helped out with the property. It was a nice place, and the living was easy. During the summer Chuck and his wife closed down the motel. They spent those three months traveling around the world or in a small mountain cabin they owned near Blowing Rock, North Carolina.

By the time Chuck was 65 he had paid off the existing mortgage and added three extra rental units by remodeling the three-bedroom apartment he and his wife had been living in. They had moved a couple of blocks away into an ocean-front condo and now had four employees that pretty much ran the motel, which was now open eleven months a year. Income had increased substantially and so had the value of the real estate under the motel. As a motel Chuck could sell it at the drop of a hat for $1,500,000 but as a site that due to its multifamily zoning could be approved for a 35-unit 10-story condominium, its worth today is likely closer to $3,000,000. Maybe even more.

But Chuck is content to live on the income that was coming in, and as he had no mortgage payment to make on either the motel or his condo, he had taken care of his retirement far more than his army retirement check could. The big hit, when he does decide to sell the site to a condominium developer, is always there when needed.

Instant Value by Design

One of the interesting factors about real estate is that a person can do something that can instantly increase the value of that property. This "something" will not be apparent unless you know where to look for it. What is this thing? Well, there are several of these things that you can do to your property or a property you want to purchase that can turn you into a millionaire. Here are two things you can do to multiply the value of your property.

Two Steps to Instant Equity Enhancement

Rezone the property to a higher economic use

Obtain a site plan approval

Rezone the Property to a Higher Economic Use: Zoning is a plan for use that governs what the authorities are bound by and that directs them as to what uses will be allowed in the various locations around the community. County governments may have a role to play in the assignment of development zones, but for the most part each city deals with its own zoning issues on its own. These zoning codes or ordinances are laws that are constantly being reviewed, challenged, and modified. The zoning for a property you own can be found illustrated on a zoning map at the city hall, usually in the Building and Zoning Department of the community where the property is located. You may also find these maps on the internet in the community web page, if they have one. All real estate investors should have these maps for each area where they look for investment potential. The zoning map is your treasure map.

As I have mentioned before, it is unlikely that you will find what the zoning is for a site on a small sign by the side of the road in front of a property you are looking at buying. Looking at the buildings that are on the site may give you a clue, as would seeing what other uses there are in the immediate area. But this is where the danger appears. What you see is not always what you need. Remember that, zoning changes, and zoning may allow a wide range of uses for the same location.

Not all uses will result in the same value. This is the basic premises of how you use zoning to your investment advantage. A run-down duplex that was built 50 years ago may have an improved economic value by being fixed up, repainted, and nicely landscaped, but the highest economic use might simply be to raze the building and construct something entirely different.

But suppose you check the zoning and, darn it, you discover a duplex is all that can be built there.

But wait a minute. You notice that a few blocks away some beautiful town-homes have been constructed, which are selling for a million dollars each. You remember that location too, and that two years ago there was nothing but similar run-down duplexes on that entire block. You pay a visit to the Planning Department of the city and discover that a developer was able to put together the entire block of property. He then filed a petition to amend the zoning to allow cluster development of town-homes on the entire block at double the density that duplexes would have provided.

The result of that proposed development had benefit to everyone. The duplex owners were able to sell their property at a higher price, the developer was able to profit handsomely from the development of million-dollar town-homes. The neighbors around that block saw their neighborhood was improving and that their own values were going up. Even the city fathers benefited, since the city was the beneficiary of a much higher tax base.

The steps for an investor to seek a zoning modification or change are not very difficult. Anyone can do it, and the actual cost is not always prohibitive. It does become expensive when the local political atmosphere is against the idea. If the local people love the idea, it is a walk in the park. Because of this, it is a good idea to become acquainted with city politics and attitudes toward development, particularly development in the area where you want to invest. If you discover a bundle of roadblocks await you, that does not mean you should stop, but it generally does mean that the battle might become expensive. How so? Well think of all those high-paid lawyers you may need to hire, and architects and traffic planners and so on, to go head to head with the city planning and zoning staff, and ultimately the city commissioners. An easier approach might be to simply ask in what parts of town would the city encourage new development. Sometimes that produces far more gold mines than diving into a prolonged fight with the very people who are capable of actually helping you.

Obtain a Site Plan Approval: Remember the three most important words in real estate: *location*, *use*, and *approval*? All three are critical to the maximum economic benefit from any real estate. Because use is governed by the zoning you either have to go with what you got, or seek to change it (see above). But then you need to get the approval to move forward. The zoning ordinance might indicate that you are allowed 50 multifamily units (apartments for example) per acre. But the city may not want 50 units built there, so they may look for legal ways to stop you. From a real estate investor's point of view, this can be a difficult task if the city has some clear-cut ways to actually stop you. Generally it is a building code, traffic problem, or fire code that can stand in your way and which becomes the wall you have to get over.

But when you approach the problem with a win-win attitude, you will discover that getting approvals, while they take time, can eventually be obtained. Developers have discovered different approaches that seem to work, depending on the community and its politics.

- *Ask for the stars but settle for the moon.* This is an approach that often works. Here the developer applies for a 60-story building on a two-acre tract of land with 300 apartments, but will agree on 30 stories and 150 apartments.

- *Schmoose the Neighbors.* This also works from time to time. Here the developer is given the challenge (often by the city Planning and Zoning Department) to make sure that any gripe of any neighbor to the project in question is dealt with before the project is presented to the city. The developer meets with the neighboring homeowners and owner associations and does his or her best to persuade them that the project will be good for the city, and even better for the neighborhood.

  Any developer who does this successfully started out on this road knowing that there will be people who will gripe and complain no matter what. Yet success will come by making a commitment to do something positive for the neighborhood. Like what? I've seen everything from donating land (which the developer might have to purchase first) for a park area, or lining the streets with shade trees, or improving roads in the area. Each homeowner and association in the neighborhood will have their own idea of what should be done.

  In the end, the developer, the neighbors, and the city come to an understanding, and the result is 150 apartments in a 25-story building. The city saves face, and the developer moves forward with a tract of land that now meets the three most important words. With the approval in hand, the developer has likely doubled or more the value of the original site.

The time it takes to change zoning or obtain a site plan approval might be a year, but for the right project it can be worth the effort. I have been part of such processes in assembling development sites for developers who then hired the team to get the approvals needed to insure that a project can be built on a given site. One simple project was a 16-unit condominium project that the zoning allowed. But the neighbors complained it was going to block their view (between two buildings) of the waterway and boats on the back side of the condos. The developer gave in to demands the neighbors wanted, to the tune of a future cost (when the development was underway) of $50,000. The city said okay too, and within three months the developer had sold the project to another developer who did not want to go through the year-long hassle. The original developer made $2,650,000 over and above his original cash invested in the deal. How much had he invested? He had contracted to buy the property for a price of $4,750,000. The terms were $1,250,000 down and $3,500,000 in financing held by the seller. But the developer didn't have to pay anything until he closed on the property. He thought he had enough time to get the approvals, but was wrong and had to give the seller $250,000 to extend the approval process time (but he would get credit for that at the closing). When he got the approvals, he had to come up with another $1,000,000 to close, and the process itself had cost him $200,000. So, by the time he closed he was actually out of pocket $1,450,000. He then sold the project to a new buyer for $7,500,000, who paid cash to the existing $3,500,000 mortgage.

Developer's Path to Near Instant Equity Increase

1.	Purchase price	$4,750,000
2.	Cost to get approval	200,000
3.	Total	$4,950,000
4.	Cash down with approvals	$1,250,000
5.	Plus cost of approval	200,000
6.	Total cash invested	$1,450,000
7.	Sale to second developer	$7,500,000
8.	Mortgage assumed	3,500,000
9.	Cash paid to original developer	$4,000,000
10.	Less original cash invested	1,450,000
11.	Developer's profit	$2,650,000

How to Build a Retirement Nest Egg the Double-Dip Way

Seeking maximum equity buildup is a good way to provide retirement income for the day when you want to sit back and relax. This means not maximizing the cash flow from the property but striking a balance that fits your day-to-day cash needs while emphasizing equity buildup. Paying off debt is essential to maximizing equity buildup. But there is more to it than just reducing debt owed against the property. A well thought-out plan that is designed to improve the property along the way is also critical. This will likely require that cash be reinvested from time to time in the form of repairs, maintenance, and improvements that will, in turn, increase the rent collections from the property. Increased rent and greater NOI is important, because that reflects in a greater cash flow potential for the next investor who will be willing to pay you far more than you had originally invested. But, in the quest for a retirement nest egg, a debt-free property can become a cash cow that supports your retirement years without your having to give up or reduce your accustomed lifestyle. Sleeping soundly at night by not worrying about the mortgage is a good feeling.

Free and clear real estate is like money in the bank, too. If you have an emergency need for cash, it is relatively easy to get cash by using it as security for a mortgage. Getting to a debt-free situation gives the property owner the ability to draw out some of that equity tax free by placing new debt on the property. Take a look at this example:

Brad purchased a strip shopping center 20 years ago for $1,500,000. It had a strong NOI of $155,000 per year, and he was able to obtain a $1,200,000 mortgage that paid off in 20 years. The terms of the mortgage were 240 installments (1 a month for 20 years) at 8 percent interest. The monthly payments were $10,167.28 per month or $122,007.00 per year. He was able to put some of the leftover cash flow back into the property every year, constantly improving the make up of tenants and the overall value of the property.

By the time he had paid off the mortgage, his NOI had grown to $310,000 per year, all of which was going directly into Brad's pocket as there was no debt service to cover. The value of the property now exceeded $3,200,000, and he decided to put a new loan on the property so he could pull out some of his equity to make other acquisitions. He found a lender more than willing to lend him $2,000,000 on the property.

During the 20 years of his ownership, he had taken a straight-line depreciation, which was the lowest depreciation he could take. His current tax basis (original cost less depreciation taken) was $700,000. This turned out to be good for him, as it would mean that he would not have any recapture of depreciation if he sold the property later on. Had he taken an accelerated depreciation, which was allowed, he would have to pay tax on 100 percent of the depreciation taken.

Brad discussed this potential with his accountant and his lawyer. Each of them reminded Brad that he had to be aware of two potential problems: tax due from the recapture of depreciation, which would not apply in this case, and the income or capital gain tax due on debt relief in excess of the tax basis of the property. As in the case of a sale of depreciable tangible property (such as equipment or furniture), the possible capital gain would be taxed at the earned income rate for the taxpayer. Real estate income that is taxable as a result of recapture of depreciation, in general, would be taxed at a special 25 percent capital gain tax rate. It is important that all investors seek a good real estate accountant in any tax matters, as there are exceptions to most rules.

Debt Relief That Exceeds the Tax Basis: This occurs when the investor has created new debt on a property and then exchanges the property for another property. If the debt on the property the taxpayer is giving up is less than the debt on the property he is receiving, there will be earned income tax due on the difference.

However, because borrowed money is not treated as income, there is no income tax due on the cash. As long as Brad kept the strip stores, the IRS could not recapture earned income on past depreciation as he had used a straight-line method, and the new debt over his basis would trigger a tax only if he sold the property without paying off the debt first.

The Seven Sources of Equity Buildup

There will be some natural correlation between the sources of equity buildup and those of cash flow. The same basic steps that an investor would make to increase income from rents would apply to both situations. The difference is in how the investor uses that revenue. If the bulk of it is diverted to other interests, such as sailing around the world, or a grander life style, then the property may suffer from not reaching its potential through continued upgrades or other improvements. The principal sources of equity buildup are as follows:

Market appreciation

The cost of living

Reduced debt service

Increased cash flow

Economic conversion potential

Better management

New income sources

Let's review these in detail.

Market Appreciation

Each piece of investment property will have a number of factors that can cause its value to go up or down. Generally the condition of the rental market for the immediate area around the property will be a governing factor. However, this may not be the sole reason for a decline of a specific property's value. Usually there are several events taking place that can make a sudden change in property values. Some of these changes are temporary, such as new road work that shuts down traffic for months at a time, to often devastating results for rental occupancy in the area. Other events are focused on some major new developments nearby that will have a major impact on the economics of the area. These can be good, such as the building of a major hospital three blocks away, or some other major employment center such as a new shopping mall or government center. Then there is the other side of the coin, the negative impact, such as a major highway that takes a right-of-way through a formerly upper-class residential area.

These events, it is nice to know, whether they have a beneficial impact or a negative one, are not overnight events. They have been in planning stages for months, sometimes years, and yet their impact for the majority of people will occur that Sunday morning when the newspaper announces that the construction for "whatever" has now begun. Smart real estate investors (of whose ranks you should strive to become a member) know all about the bureaucratic process and have been following the events as they unfolded, since the embryonic moments of the formation of the event.

Real estate follows predictable patterns, only not always in a universal way. By this I mean that in every part of town, every kind and category of real estate will go through predictable stages of value increase and decrease. However, these categories of real estate do not start a cycle at the same time; you must look closer to what causes certain categories of real estate to go up or down in value. In addition, even the same category may be rising in one area of town and falling in another. Let's take midsize multifamily rental apartment buildings as an example. This category of real estate will depend on a multitude of circumstances, none of which may appear in the same mix in the neighboring city, or across the country, or in the next cycle. Let's examine this single category for a moment in the hope that a detailed study will give you a clear picture of how these cycles work.

A Multifamily Real Estate Category Cycle of Value Increase and Decrease: Okay, here is a list of seven situations and circumstances that will effect the value of rental apartments (as well as other categories of real estate, but often not for the same reason).

Keep in mind that there are likely other situations and circumstances that may be unique to your area. The important thing is to learn what does effect values in your area and to learn how to apply them to the category of real estate that you may want to acquire. Each of these following items will relate to the market area of the real estate in question.

Employment Conditions: Is employment running at a high level? Or are there a lot of people in the area out of work? This will have the most dramatic effect on rental apartments when there is a sudden change in this situation. If there are only a few major employment centers in the area and one or more of them suddenly are shut down, then there can be an overnight panic in the working class of people who make up the majority of the economic impact for the community. Clearly, if we are talking about Microsoft, the impact would be on a much higher level if it suddenly was shut down (because Bill Gates decided to shuck it and move to Vanuatu or some other such place), than if Famous Amos cookies factory had to lay off all its bakers and such because of a butter shortage.

Communities that rely on any employment centers that are connected, such as Boeing and all its subcontractors, or theme parks and hotels that house the millions of tourists that visit them can be greatly affected by outside events. A sudden downward change in travel patterns, such as occurred immediately following the twin-towers attack caused wide spread layoffs of thousands of tourist-oriented labor. That in turn created sudden vacancy levels in rental apartments as workers scrambled to relocate to other areas where jobs could be found.

Category and Demographics of Retired People: Virtually every area has a mix of people by age, percentage of children, students, workers, and retired people. The workers are the only important factor of this mix that will also include unemployed. But one of the stabilizing factors of this mix is the nature of the retired people who also live in the area. If the community has a large retired population that is mostly living on social security and modest pensions, then this community will not have the same economic potential as an affluent retired community of multi-millionaires. There are companies that provide very accurate statistics on the demographics of virtually every area in the country. You will find these sources via the internet. A print out of the make-up of residents in the areas you define can provide you with age groups, income levels, values of homes, and more helpful information.

The Direction of Growth: The economic stability of a community is a factor that lenders as well as developers look to in their long-range planning. Because of this, growth tends to promote more growth. Cities that can grow in every direction generally will have the greatest traffic routes that connect with other employment centers. Where it is easy to identify these traffic routes, it is easy to anticipate areas that will experience new growth the fastest. The idea that you invest in areas that grow from both ends to the middle is a very practical investment strategy. It doesn't take long to figure this out, because all it takes is a current map and a visit to the county and state departments of transportation to ascertain what their future planning has in store for the area. Then take a drive around the community.

Many cities cannot grow in all directions. Cities that front lakes, oceans, or rivers, for example, have their growth channeled to limited areas. Florida, as an example, has this situation, since cities along the Atlantic and Gulf coast are very restricted as to where growth can take place. From Lake Okeechobee south to the southern part of Miami, the everglades becomes a barrier for growth through the center of South Florida, forcing growth to be in relatively narrow swatches that hug the two coasts. This kind of situation can be found in other parts of the world, too.

Infrastructure Changes: Any change in infrastructure can have impacts to real estate values, as I have illustrated earlier. As for multifamily rental properties, the impact can be strong when any of those changes create a demand for real estate that can diminish the availability of existing rental properties, while at the same time hamper the new development of rental properties.

Political Thrust Toward New Development: All states in the United States have a department whose principal objective is to attract employment centers to that state. Counties and cities within those states also compete with each other for these sources of jobs because it is logical that jobs promote growth. But not all jobs are equal, and the sources for high paying jobs, such as Microsoft or medical, banking, or marketing centers are not so abundant, and often the jobs that are available tend to be more service-oriented. The thousands of jobs in New York City that are found in hotels, restaurants are generally at the lower end of the pay scale, and living space for many of these employees is not available in the immediate area. This forces these employees out of the area, which has the reverse impact. This occurs because the money is spent outside the area where it is earned. Although this does not seem to have a negative impact on New York City, it can create problems for other areas of the world. Acapulco, Mexico, for example is full of tourist accommodations and services. Therefore, in the immediate area where these facilities exist there is a surreal atmosphere of wealth that quickly disappears to a near-poverty level in the matter of a few city blocks away from the wealthy tourist area.

How the employment aspect of the area in which you want to invest is or can be affected by employment and the growth patterns will be very important to your long-range investment thinking.

Supply and Demand: Most categories of real estate function on a supply and demand rotation. It doesn't really matter which comes first, you can pretty much depend on the other following. The length of the time period between the two is the secret that every investor wishes to possess. There are keys to this secret, of course, depending on the category of real estate in question. Industrial or heavy commercial categories are relatively easy to follow, because they are generally one of the least available categories in any area, and they are usually the most visible where they are found. Here zoning plays an important role because industrial or heavy commercial uses are often confined to parts of a city that are the most distant from upper-scale residential. This is either by natural design of the growth of the city where you find industrial areas next to the ports or rail lines that prompted their location in the first place, or through relocation to more distant areas as the inner-city industrial areas were absorbed into a growing city and put to use, by rezoning and urban redevelopment. Seattle, Washington, and Pittsburgh, Pennsylvania, are two good examples of where this has occurred. Developers and investors can easily identify situations that are ripe for similar redevelopment. In this instance, the developers would take advantage of supplying a property that is in demand, such as high-priced down-town or near-town condominiums, and create locations through redevelopment of older areas that experience a decline in demand for their existing uses.

Rising Development Costs: Development costs generally have a steady increase tied to the cost of living. That is, as prices of materials rise, the cost to assemble those materials does as well. However, development costs can have spikes that are tied to events that are temporary. The worldwide demand for steel or concrete or lumber needed to rebuild cities, as the result of some catastrophic event, can be the cause for this temporary rise. Those same events have a double whammy on the increase in cost as it effects the employment cycles of an area. Where there is a lot of development going on, there usually is a shortage in skilled construction labor.

Rising development costs are not limited to the construction aspect of a category of real estate. Included in the overall cost to build new product is the cost of the land, the soft costs that include planning and design, financing costs, and the overhead of the total operation. Marketing costs are generally a fixed percentage of the overall cost, so that too contributes to the increased investment.

The Cost of Living

The United States Department of Labor (www.bls.gov) provides free information on many interesting topics. One of the most useful in real estate is its cost of living indexes. Go to the web page shown above and click on the appropriate index or data base you want to review. The cost of living indexes are shown in the upper left corner of the web page text.

Cost of living is compiled through an elaborate process of data taking. Most leases and many contracts call for application of one or more of these indexes. I personally use the "All Items" index for periodic rent increases. You can check out these different indexes and discover how to use them on line.

Cost of living is a fact, and although not all the items go up, the overall "all items" index generally does. The continual rise in the cost of living works to the real estate investor's advantage, particularly when obtaining leverage through application of debt. Review the following example.

Leverage and Its Friend, the Cost of Living

The long-term mortgage that is available for most any real estate investment can be the instrument of leverage for real estate investors. Because its repayment is made by the tenants of a property at a fixed level, which, if it is not an adjustable rate mortgage, does not increase due to any rise in the cost of living. On the other hand, the rent paid by tenants will generally rise due to the effect of the cost of living. If increases in expenses do not exceed the increase in the lease, that increase will go straight to the NOI of the property and not be diminished by the fixed debt service. Let me illustrate this in the following example.

Julie purchases an office building for $3,126,906 and pays $1,371,820 in cash as her down payment and assumes the existing mortgage of $1,755,086. The building has seven tenants. They each pay $3,000 a month in base rent plus $1,000 in CAM. Because the CAM covers all the expenses of the building, including management and reserves, let's only look at the base rent which is her net cash flow before debt service. Julie has a first mortgage on the property that requires her to pay $11,854 a month of principal and interest (P&I). (This would be a $1,755,086 mortgage for 28 years at 7 percent interest). The property has a cash flow, as is shown on the next page, that returns Julie approximately 8 percent in pre-tax income.

Calculate the Cash Flow Before Income Tax

Base rent: $3,000 × 7 = $21,000 per month × 12 =	$252,000
Common area maintenance: $1,000 × 7 × 12 =	84,000
Total collections from tenants	$336,000
Total expenses of the property	84,000
Net operating income	$252,000
Debt service for the year ($11,854 × 12)	142,255
Annual cash flow before income tax	$109,745

Assuming that for the past five years the cost of living has increased by just under 4 percent per year, the new NOI would be $302,000.

Cost of Living Increase in Leases over 5 Years

Base rent increases by 20 percent (compound of less than 4 percent per year)

Base rent at start of the example	$252,000
Apply cost of living increases	× 1.20
New net operating income	$302,400
Less debt service	142,255
Cash flow before taxes	$160,145

Julie decides to sell at the end of the fifth year, and the investment return rate desired by a new owner is 8 percent, and nothing else has changed in the economics of the building except that the base rent has been increased each year according to a cost of living index. As was shown above, that index had increased by a total of 20 percent over the five-year period. The current mortgage balance owed would now be $1,639,392, and the new buyer would either pay off at closing or assume it.

By now the property has a current cash flow before taxes of $160,145. The investor wants to generate the same 8 percent return (as did Julie when she purchased the property) and is willing to pay cash to the existing debt. To resolve how much he needs to come up with to close, all we have to do is to calculate how much money he needs to invest so that the current cash flow ($160,145) will be his 8 percent return. We would then add to that the existing mortgage the buyer will assume to get his total purchase price.

Keep in mind that if the investor were to refinance to a larger mortgage at any rate below 8 percent interest there would be positive leverage in its favor, and the return would be greater than the demanded 8 percent. However, the point of this example is to show what happens solely because of the cost of living increase. To do this accurately, both Julie and the new investor expected to earn 8 percent cash flow before income taxes. So, we calculate the down payment based on an 8 percent return on the cash flow the property is producing at the moment of the sale.

Down payment: $160,145 ÷ 8 percent = $2,001,812

In this instance, the buyer could assume the existing debt, which has 23 years remaining of $1,639,392. Or, if the investor could borrow more at a lower interest rate than the 8 percent CAP rate the yield on the investment would be leveraged up to a higher return.

New Investor's down payment	$2,001,812
Assumption of the existing loan	1,639,392
Total price an investor would pay	$3,641,204

Calculate Julie's Cash Flow from New Equity Buildup at the Closing of the Sale:
The overall price paid by the buyer is not really a factor here; all we have to do is look at what Julie puts in her pocket (before income tax) after deducting the total cash she

paid out when she purchased the property. The investor is buying a cash flow of $160,145 with the hope that the cash flow will increase just as it did for Julie. Naturally, there could be many other factors that could cause the new value to climb to a new plateau, no matter what happened to the cost of living.

Amount paid to Julie by the buyer of her office building	$2,001,812
Less her down payment when she purchased the property	1,371,820
Total amount of profit (new equity in the property)	$ 629,992

Okay, so in five years with an overall average base rent increase of 20 percent, Julie has created new equity of $629,992 in the property. This new equity is equal to over 45 percent of her original cash invested of $1,371,820. If the equity increased 45 percent in five years and the only thing that changed was a five–year cost of living increase of 20 percent, what magic is going on? You need to think about this for a moment. The cost of living went up 20 percent over five years yet her equity went up 45+%. What caused this paradox to occur?

The key here is to realize that small changes that affect the cash flow have a much larger effect on the equity in the property. An increase in cash flow of $10,000 for the year would, in the 8 percent example shown here, will bump up equity by $125,000. This occurs because an 8 percent return on $125,000 invested is $10,000.

In Julie's example, all we did was let the cost of living increase provision in the leases cause the collectable income to rise. Coupling that with other changes in the cash flow would have the same effect. Refinanced debt at a lower rate, reduced real estate taxes or insurance, anything at all that puts more cash in the investor's pocket will have this effect. But be careful of the other side of this coin. Lose $10,000 in cash flow for any reason and the investors will discount the value, and the equity quicker than you can say, "ouch."

Reduced Debt Service

We have seen several examples of how reduced debt service can increase cash flow. The insider tricks that make this work, first for increased cash flow, then to generate a higher price (increased equity) at the time the property is sold, are limited by the investor's ability to borrow funds at the most favorable terms. We have seen what happens with an interest-only mortgage. Of all the techniques the mortgage that leaves the maximum amount of rent in the hands of the buyer would be the zero coupon mortgage. Here is a simple example of how this works.

Zero Coupon Mortgage: A zero coupon mortgage is when neither the interest nor the principal is paid for a period of time. This period can be whatever the parties can agree to and is best (and easiest) when the seller holds the mortgage. Why the seller? Because the seller is motivated to sell the property, so there are benefits that go to the seller that can be satisfied. A bank lender is not so motivated. They want to get their interest and principal payments. Keep in mind, though, it may be effective if the seller holds a portion of the transaction as a second mortgage.

Zackery negotiated to purchase the four unit apartment complex I introduced to you as Investment Property Number One in Chapter 1 (see the property offering that is shown on page 36).

The price is $370,000, and Zackery knows that he can go to a local savings and loan institution and borrow $296,000. The loan terms would be set with a 40-year amortization schedule, 7 percent interest on the balances outstanding, with a monthly payment of $1,868.00 a month ($22,416.00 a year). The lender will balloon the mortgage at the end of 15 years, which means that at the end of 15 years Zackery, or whoever owns the property at that time has assumed the mortgage, would be obliged to pay off the mortgage. The balloon payment, or better said, the amount of principal that is still owed at the end of 15 years would be $251,010.

At this juncture, Zackery would have to invest the balance above the $296,000 mortgage to meet the seller's asking price of $370,000. This would put the mortgage amount to be 80 percent of the purchase price. The loan to value ratio of 80/20 is generally available for this type of investment if the lenders like the property and the borrower.

Price	$370,000
Mortgage	296,000
Down payment	$ 74,000

Review the income and expense for this property. If you double check back to Chapter 1, you will notice that the income has been improved slightly. With the debt service Zackery has been offered by the savings and loan institution, his cash flow would return to him 6.6 percent on his invested cash. The goal is to see what he can do to bring that investment up without changing the price, income, or expenses.

Zackery's Anticipated Income and Expenses

Income Collected	*Annual*
(3) One-bedroom units at $800.00 per month	$28,800.00
(1) Two-bedroom unit at $1,150.00 per month	13,800.00
Laundry revenue from coin op. machines	964.00
A. Total Annual Income Collections	$43,564.00
B. Expenses for the Year	
Accounting (year-end tax report)	$ 250.00
Property insurance	2,300.00
Property tax	4,895.00

Water, sewer, electricity charges	2,510.00
Repairs and replacements	1,500.00
Building maintenance	1,800.00
Management	2,000.00
Misc. expenses	1,000.00
C. Total Annual Expenses	$16,255.00
Total net operating income (NOI) for the year	$27,309.00
Less debt service	22,416,00
Cash flow before income taxes	$ 4,893.00

If the property was free and clear of any existing debt, the seller might be enticed to hold a new first mortgage, but let's assume that this is not the case as there is existing debt of $200,000 on the property, which Zackery will pay off. But what if Zackery offers the seller a zero coupon mortgage at 7.5 percent that balloons in six years with the original face amount of $50,000. Zackery then splits the $50,000 into two amounts, $40,000 that he takes off the bank loan bringing that down from $296,000 to $256,000. The other $10,000 he takes off the down payment, reducing it from $74,000 to $64,000. Here is what the transaction looks like now:

Price	$370,000
First mortgage	$256,000
Second mortgage	50,000
Down payment	64,000
Purchase price	$370,000

By reducing the loan to a 70 percent loan to value ratio, the savings and loan agreed to drop the interest rate to 6.5 percent. This would drop the monthly payment to $1,532 a month or $18,384 for the year. Let's see how the investment shapes up now:

Net operating income	$27,309
Less	
First mortgage annual debt service	$18,384
Second mortgage is zero payment for six years	0
Revised cash flow before income tax	$ 8,925
Invested cash	$64,000
New return ($8,925 ÷ $64,000)	13.9%

At the end of six years Zackery's second mortgage would balloon. He should monitor his progress in getting the rents up, but as we have seen, the cost of living alone will go a long way to do that. His $50,000 zero coupon mortgage at 7.5 percent will now have a principal (plus interest) due of $83,614. Since his overall goal was to maximize his equity buildup, it might appear that he is going in the wrong direction because he now owes more than he did when he closed on the property. But if he continually reinvested cash into the building to improve it, he could anticipate increasing rents more than enough to allow him to refinance the property on or before the end of the sixth year to cover the balloon and to maintain the cash flow balance that works for him.

Zackery could also chose to settle on a cash flow of 7 percent of his $64,000 investment and keep $4,480 of the $8,925 the property is returning to him. The balance of $4,445 could be used to reduce the balance on either, or both, of the mortgages, although the likely choice would be to retire as much as possible of the second mortgage, since it is at the higher interest rate.

Increased Cash Flow

Because cash flow is the result of income less expenses and debt service, any change that increases income and/or reduces expenses and/or debt service will achieve the same goal of boosting the bottom line, which is your cash flow before income taxes. But keep this in mind. It is okay to increase expenses and even debt service if the over-all increase in income exceeds that increase.

Economic Conversion Potential

It is my opinion that for many investors the highest investment return will come from economic conversion potentials. Here the investor acquires a property, then converts it to a greater income producing investment. This might be a rental apartment building that is converted into a residential condo, or a medical office building, or an old motel that becomes executive suites, or a condo-hotel, or a used car lot that becomes a new car dealership. The opportunities are endless. The key to success in this kind of venture is to know what the existing zoning will allow, as well as what potential other zoning may exist. In this second scenario the potential other zoning will, to a major degree, depend on the whims of the planning and zoning department of the community and the political view toward development in that part of town.

There are drawbacks to economic development that will become evident the moment an investor begins to shape the business plan for the venture. First of all, virtually any conversion requires time, building renovations, plans for those renovations, and a loss of revenue during the actual conversion period. All of this costs money and can be a major part of the investment.

If the project, however, has a strong potential for return, lenders understand what is going on and look to the finished value of the newly converted investment as the basis for mortgage funding. Based on the strength and experience of the investor in such conversions and net worth, financing can usually be arranged to support the acquisition, planning, redevelopment, and sales (or rent-up) stages of the project. Investors build into the loan request the debt service that is needed to take them through to the moment when income from sales or rents begin to flow.

Conversion of rental properties to owned properties is one of the first kinds of economic conversions that investors should review. In doing this it is a good idea to have an escape plan to a higher priced rental just in case sales of the end product do not measure up to the projected price point to give the investor the return that he or she wanted.

Throughout this book I will touch on these economic conversions as a way of life. Sometimes, as we have already seen, the investor does not actually carry through with the conversion, but instead gets all the approvals and then sells the basket of location, new use, and approvals to the developer who carries the project on to completion.

Better Management

Any income producing real estate will have certain levels of management connected to it. While it is possible to hire such management, a hands-on approach can produce substantial results. There will be a trade-off, however, anytime you expect to manage your own investments. That trade-off comes from the loss of the time that you must devote to the management of the property. Many real estate investors take that in stride and do not assign a dollar value to their own time. After all, they rationalize, I would rather be working for myself than someone else. Okay, but what are you worth? Would it be better to have a full-time property manager whom you pay $40,000 a year while you work part-time (at something you like doing more than dealing with tenants) and get paid $70,000 a year?

The answers to those two questions are for you to answer to yourself. And what you do with the resulting information is equally private. A good friend of mine, and the co-founder of one of the largest motel chains in the United States is one of the hardest-working men I have ever known. He spends at least three days a week on the road visiting his hotels and motels. His properties produce a far greater income than his competition in the areas where his properties are located. But it is at a price of his time.

What else would I do? He would reply whenever I ask him about that situation.

Another friend and client is also in the hotel business, and he too is a work fiend. But he sits back and oversees one of the best second-tier management teams I have ever seen. Still he is hands on.

Other clients of mine are off doing whatever they want. They paid their dues by learning the business from the ground up, and worked the property until they were making enough money to employ people to work for them. They knew how to hire the right people rather than to turn the properties over to management companies. But they are still experienced in the operation at hand. Simply by looking at the monthly reports their managers send to them, it only takes them a few minutes to spot a tender spot getting ready to bud into a full-blown problem.

What is the point here? Simply this. Never look in the window of the store and think that its operation is easy and simple until you have worked there. If you are buying a property that requires some skills that you never had to use, then spend some advance time learning what those skills are. Chuck, whom you have already met in this chapter, retired from the Army and bought a 17-unit motel. Did he jump from the Army right into the hospitality business? No. He worked for a year and a half for a hotel company. He started as manager of the housekeeping and maintenance department, and before he left to go it on his own, he was manager of the front desk.

Good management can make a difference between a rental property that has good, paying tenants. If you have not yet become a real estate investor, then take stock of what talents you have. Management may not be the skill you are best at, but there are many other skills that fit together nicely with real estate. Are you a good painter or carpenter? Can you fix just about anything, or lay carpet, or are you a great decorator? Any of these skills can put you into some slot of real estate management. More often than not, the biggest problem a property manager has is where is he or she going to find a plumber on Sunday afternoon. If that is your skill, then that management decision would be a snap for you. If you are like Chuck and are retired, invest some time in night courses in front desk operations or business accounting, or develop other skills that will become important when you invest in real estate. Go to work for such a company, as did Chuck. It will pay off for you in the end.

New Income Sources

Even in what looks like a shopping center full of tenants with no vacancy in sight, there can be opportunities to generate additional income. Not all of the list of items that I will shortly give you will work for all situations, and there are likely many sources not listed in this section. What I want to do is to encourage you to be observant of what is going on in the community that would fit for your property. Remember, generate an extra $10,000 in revenue over a year, and you might increase the value of your property by $125,000 for each of those ten-thousand-dollar blocks.

Antenna Space for Rent: Radio, TV, microwave, and cell phone companies all need antenna space. It doesn't take up much space, and might be allowed in an area that no one has access to except those who service the equipment. They can pay good rent, too.

Highway or Roadside Billboards: These come in a wide range of sizes, and the bigger they are the more rent you can collect. In communities that will let them go way up into the air, a place you thought would be worthless can expose the sign to a major highway just on the other side of those trees at the back of your property.

Glass-Covered Poster Areas: A nicely framed area, with glass doors over the poster areas here and there in a commercial setting, will attract people who shop or do business in the area. They can also attract people who will pay to put up a poster advertising their company, a play down the street, or an event next month. The glass doors keep the posters from being marked up or stolen, and let you keep out unwanted posters and advertisements.

Parking Lot Uses: There may be times when your parking lot is not used at all or only partially used. If the time is on a weekend (either or both Saturday and Sunday), there might be a bundle of extra income that can be made from opening the lot to a wide range of events. How about Hobby Time, a four-hour timeslot once a month where hobby enthusiasts can bring their motorized cars, trucks, and so on to display, race, and sell; or Collector's Day, like every Sunday in Madrid, Spain in the Plaza Major, where collectors of just about anything you can put in a cigar box show up and set up card tables of the things they collect, buy, and sell. It's really great for all the restaurants in the Plaza too.

Antique Car Club Display; Pet Owners Day; Car, RV, and Boat Sales Day—all will have a draw, and if those are generally slow times of your property's week, then there might be added revenue there too.

Green Space: Is there a lot of green space around your property? Why not make a deal with a landscape grower to use the area for growing plants. It could make your space more attractive and generate more revenue, as well as clients for the other tenants there.

If you have out parcels that are not ready to be developed yet, how about trying any of the above for them, or plant a U-Pick it Zone on which you can get a couple crops a year to let people come and pick their own strawberries, corn, peppers, or whatever grows best in your area.

Building equity is easy when you work at it. Having pride in the ownership makes the work fun because you get to see the economic benefits of your effort. The key to building equity is to continue to upgrade the property as well as the tenants. As rents increase, you can continue to spend a portion of the extra income to continue the improvement, which in turn helps you keep good tenants.

CHAPTER 3

How to Find Properties with Great Cash Flow and/or Equity Buildup Potential

The goal of this chapter is:

To Show Tips and Traps of Finding Properties that Maximize Your Goals

Getting Ready to Invest in Real Estate

There is some good news here. You are not born a real estate investor, nobody is. This means that even if you are just thinking about investing in real estate, there is an opportunity awaiting you if you follow the rules that thousands of successful investors have perfected. Investing in real estate is an acquired talent. Yet, like the roll of dice in Vegas, it may bring you fortunes virtually by accident. There is often what might seem like plain darn good luck, but, more likely, you are starting to see opportunities you never realized existed before. Continued success and great wealth through investing in anything comes from a thorough knowledge of the element of interest and not from darn good luck. Therefore, I designed this chapter to open a number of mental doors that you need to become acquainted with about the rules of the real estate game.

By the time you have completed this book you will already be able to spot real opportunities of property that can produce a profit within your own neighborhood. You might even be living next to one such property now and not see the signs that will tell you, later, that this is a property worth buying.

It never ceases to thrill me how this process works. It is all in seeing the hidden elements of property and learning how to become familiar with the trends that any neighborhood may go through.

Nevertheless, buying real estate is a very personal kind of investment. It has the ability to help investors attain goals that, as I have indicated earlier, vary between investors. The same property can take each investor to those different goals based on how they have structured the transaction. The following are several elements that you need to know.

Review each in detail.

Terms and Concepts You Need to Know

Lenders' Preferences
Comfort Zone Investing
Local Zoning and Politics

Lenders' Preferences

Every lender has a predetermined ideal loan. Occasionally that loan opportunity is presented to that lender. Nevertheless, this is a rare event, since most loans are made to borrowers for situations and are secured by real estate that does not fit the exact criteria of that ideal loan. However, the closer the borrower can get to that ideal loan situation the better the likelihood of getting the loan.

Assume you own a vacant commercial lot and it has increased substantially in value over the 15 years you have owned it. You now decide that you can use the built up equity as collateral to build on the lot. You check around with some lenders and discover that commercial loans are being made at the lowest interest rate in 10 years or more. Now is the time for you to act. But what should you build?

You decide it would be nice to own a flag hotel, so you contact several hotel companies, and one of them is happy to offer you a franchise for that location. You go to the bank you have dealt with forever to get the loan and are surprised that the loan you are offered is at terms that are far more costly than what you had anticipated. You shop around, and guess what? Every one of the loan offers you get is even more costly than the first.

So, you back up, go back to the first lender, and ask what is going on? They tell you that the bank does not like hotels. Then they add, "Why not build something like an office building. After all, there is a shortage of well-located office space, whereas, the only hotels around town that are doing well are out by the Interstate, some 10 miles away."

The moral of this story is don't even think of doing anything that will need financing until you get the pulse on what the local lenders like. If you play the game they like, you will find them far more willing lending partners in your many future ventures.

Comfort Zone Investing

This is what I believe is the very best pattern to follow when investing in anything, and most certainly real estate. To understand exactly how effective this concept is, let us look at two of the more common methods that investors use to locate property to purchase.

Follow the Leader: This is where the real estate investor goes around looking for good buys that all the other investors seem to be buying. This form of investing, while sometimes successful is without any concentrated direction, due diligence, and certainly not much homework in what controls the values in the area. This kind of investor listens for the pulse of what is going on, reads the newspapers, and may even attend zoning and commission meetings in the area. When the investor hears that strip stores are hot, he or she contacts several real estate agents, all of whom are happy to sell this investor whatever is listed in the local multiple listing service.

One of these agents brings him a listing that is directly across the street from a center that had sold a year ago for $55.00 a square foot (say 15,000 square feet of rental space, which sold then for $825,000). The agent says that the new owner painted the building and put it back on the market for $1,300,000 and it sold in two weeks. Now here, the agent says, is another center right across the street in the same condition that can be purchased for $50.00 a square foot.

The investor rushes out and sure enough, his offer of $48.00 per square foot is accepted. Three months after the closing of the center, when the repainting of the newly purchased property was finished, the investor discovered that the center across the street, which was sold for a huge profit, was in another city, a city with very liberal zoning ordinances. On the other hand, the city where his capital is now invested is very restrictive. Their building codes require twice the amount of parking per square foot of building than the code of the other city across the street. This means that either less square footage can be built, or that a parking garage may be needed to support the desired size of building. The result of this is a much greater cost per rentable square footage. In turn, this means a far more difficult time in store for this new investor to rent up at a NOI that will support a higher cost.

The Shotgun: This is a typical approach to real estate investing of most novices, and like the follow the leader technique, it will involve a lot of work. Here the investor has selected an area in which to invest, which is generally too big and often made up of a number of cities or even several counties. In this scenario, the investor scours the area looking at property that is for sale, trying to find that right property to purchase. Like the follow the leader, this method occasionally can turn up a good buy, but it is unlikely that the investor will recognize just how good it is. The overwhelming task of understanding the zoning rules and regulations in several different cities makes that task nearly impossible. Okay, now lets look at the comfort zone method of locating property to buy.

The Comfort Zone: This is your sweet spot that you have selected because it is already partially (at least) familiar to you. It might be your neighborhood or the part of town where you live or work, or both. Initially it will be totally within one city, so you do not have to divide yourself between zoning rules and regulations of other cities. You need meet only one set of officials for each of the important areas of local government.

Once you apply the necessary steps to fine tuning your knowledge of this area, you will soon be an expert on what happens in this zone. Best of all, because you will also know everything about the zoning and building codes that are applicable to this zone, you will begin to see the hidden aspects that make one property a better investment than the one across the street, or even right next door.

Your real estate comfort zone will build your confidence in real estate as an investment in and for the future.

Local Zoning and Politics

There are many things about the politics of a community that affect the ultimate value of real estate within that community. Of them all, the following are the most important for you to understand and then to use.

Development orientation

Building and zoning structure

Let's look at each of these in detail.

Development Orientation: How does the political leadership feel about real estate development? Are they for it or against it? The nicest part of this is that all it takes is a visit to a couple of commission meetings to find out. If the majority of the commission tends to pick at every new project that is presented to them for approval and more would-be new projects are turned down than approved, then it would be safe to say the city is stacked against the developers.

If you are still not sure of the political orientation, talk to several architects you will meet at project presentations before the Planning Department meetings or even the Commission meetings. They will tell you exactly how things are in this city. Oh, be sure to ask if there is another city in the general area that is pro development. If there is, then you may want to take a look at real estate opportunities there. Why? It is all a matter of economics and time.

The cost to get a new project approved is sharply increasing and taking longer than anyone ever thought. In some cities that I am acquainted with, it can take a year to work your way through all the steps necessary from site plan approval to approval of building plans. It is not unusual for a developer to spend thousands of dollars in this process only to get shot down at the final city commission meeting because a neighboring home owner association objected to a shadow or the color of the proposed building or some other item about the project. Even though the zoning allows that color or shadow, most city commissioners are easily persuaded by voters to say no to anything that upsets those voters.

Often the zoning ordinances are written in such a way that the city fathers have the right to stop anything that is inconsistent with the nature of a neighborhood. The term sometimes written into the ordinance is "incompatible development" or other words that mean the same thing. This makes urban renewal very difficult, and if the neighborhood is over 40 years old, it is hard to have anything new come into the area and still be "compatible."

Be very cautious about investing in areas where the political deck is stacked against real estate development. You may have to wait until the voters realize what is going on and bring about a change.

Building and Zoning Structure: This goes along with the political attitude of a community because the local governing officials are the ones who can enact new zoning and building codes. If the political structure is sour toward new development, then you can bet that the building and zoning structure will be tough to live with.

In many cities, the zoning and/or building codes seem to be constantly in review. They use terms like "re-zoning in progress," or "zoning in review." What I mean is a developer may not know exactly what the zoning or building codes will be by the time his project gets to the final meeting, where it might be approved or shot down. If you think this sounds illogical, it most certainly is, but here is how it works.

Parker is a developer who has negotiated to buy a three-acre tract of land where he wants to build condominium apartments. At the time he goes to contract, the zoning allows him to build 50 multifamily units per acre and to build 20 floors in height. So, he brings together a development team that consists of an architect, the necessary engineers, lawyers, and other consultants to provide the required studies the city will ask for during the presentation. The project starts its process with an informal meeting with several (or all) of the officials of the Development Review Committee (DRC). They go over the rules and regulations that will apply in the approval process and what they will want to see in the way of design. Most cities have some theme they encourage, and heaven help the developer who does not follow that theme.

The team gets to work and after considerable time, which can be months for large projects, the formal DRC meeting is held and a comprehensive plan is presented to them by the developer and his team. Now the members of the DRC deliberate, and after a week or more a DRC report is returned to the developer. In this report, each member of the DRC will list what he or she did not like (and therefore won't approve) and usually offer suggestions as to how to get that needed approval from that member. These members are usually paid staff from the building and zoning departments and control at least the following areas (and probably more, depending on the city and its geographic location): traffic, utility installations, dry area storm water retention, fire controls and adherence to fire codes, electrical, and plumbing installations, parking facilities, landscaping, aesthetics, and so on.

All the developer has to do to move on is to accept all the recommendations, or battle out some agreed-to concession. The developer then moves to the Planning Department Meeting, where the heads of the planning board meet to hear the developer's presentation. This is where the public gives their input, which is usually negative. There may be some people who voice approval too, but these are often subcontractors or the employees or friends of the developer. Often, more concessions from the developer are asked for by the members who will be voting on the project. The developer anticipates the need to give some concessions, since they pave the way toward an approval vote, and allow the authorities some brownie points with the objecting public.

At this point, the project can be approved or turned down. If turned down, the developer can generally gamble and take it all the way to the city commission where the commission members can overrule the Planning Department. If the Planning Department did approve the project, it will go ahead to the next step; that is, unless the commission (all it takes is one commissioner) decides to have it come before the commission for final approval.

Assume that the final approval is given; now the developer can proceed with his design team to complete the plans for presentation to the building department for their final approval. At this point, the project is moving forward toward development.

But wait. Remember the zoning was originally announced as "in progress or in development." What if the review changes the density from 50 units per acre down to 35 units per acre? If the developer has designed for 50 units per acre and the change happens before that final approval, he or she may have a battle ahead to actually get that final approval.

Because of this kind of bureaucratic mess, most developers protect themselves to some degree by having an out clause in their contract that gives them the right to withdraw from the purchase agreement in such a turn of events. But what about the thousands of dollars spent to get to that stage. The developer has to kiss that money and time good-bye. And of course, the seller of the land, loses his time and the deal. Worse still, the property may lose value due to the reduced development density.

Real estate investors need to keep a watchful eye on the local political establishment and their staffs. It is so easy to slowly pick away a property owner's rights by removing the flexibility of use of real estate. A change in set backs that suddenly eliminate the opportunity to add a second bedroom, or a reduced density, which now will not allow the five-unit apartment building, for which you purchased the property, in the first place, may take value away from your property.

How to Decide What You Want to Buy

One of the greatest difficulties for someone starting out in real estate is to decide what to buy. It is easy to see people making money with almost any category of real estate at almost any time. The problem with this is that it can be hard to grasp the fact that people do lose money investing in real estate.

The first rule of investing (in anything), is to have as much knowledge about the category of the investment as possible and to have some special talent that enables you to add value to whatever investment that is. Want to invest in diamonds, then get to know them like your own kidney stones, because if you make a mistake it will feel like you are passing one (a diamond that is). The same advice about being knowledgable about the investment works for real estate just as it does for anything. The only difference with real estate over most investments is that you can make a difference between the investment being successful and profitable or a bust. Sorry, but the stock market runs its own course, and there is little you can do after you have made the investment except hope that your broker was right, or that your advance study of the stock and the market around it proves to be worthwhile.

Okay, real estate is a vast enterprise and because it is so unique from place to place, it is so very important that you start slowly and get your feet wet in the business. Because of this, it is important that you look at the downside to every property as well as the upside potentials. Examine the pros and cons of the following investment properties.

Rental Apartments

The residential rental apartment market has its difficulties, but there is a special advantage to this kind of investment when the circumstances are right.

First of all, there are several kinds of people who are attracted to the idea of renting instead of owning. It is not just the economics of not having enough money to purchase a home or condo, although that does enter into the picture for many would-be property owners who are forced to rent because their economic situation does not support property ownership.

The best situation for rental apartments, as an investment, would be in locations where there is a high employment of middle-range salaries and the source of employees is young to middle-aged people. By middle-range employment, I mean that the salaries, whatever they are, are just below the comfort level for the renter to become an owner. Clearly, both the rental market and ownership market in Savanna, Georgia, will be softer (less expensive) than in New York City, but then, the wages in expensive areas somewhat compensate for that situation.

In many areas of the country, rental apartment facilities are large complexes, some of which are gated communities that cater to active people. In other parts of the country, investors can find smaller buildings that may range from 4 or 5 apartments to 100 units. Each category of apartment complex can be a good investment, and the larger, more upscale developments generally will support their own management. As with any kind of real estate, management may be a limiting factor in your choice for what you want to own.

Small apartment complexes are ideal as a starter investment when the investor lives in one of the apartments and rents out the others. This is exactly how I started investing in real estate, and I still own the first such apartment building I developed and lived in for four years.

The biggest advantage in apartment rentals, however, is the future conversion of the property from a rental to a condominium, or co-op residential apartment building.

These conversions seem to run in cycles where developers will come in and convert most of the rentals in the area into condominiums, which causes a shortage in rentals, which is filled by new rental complexes being built. There is a lull for a while; then the converters come back to town and start all over again. I will touch on conversions in a moment.

I recommend all first-time real estate investors to take whatever steps are necessary to stop being renters themselves. In essence, get out of the cycle of helping other people get rich. Stop paying rent if at all possible. How do you do this? Buy a property that is a combination of your "home" and additional rental apartments that have tenants who give you cash flow as well as paying the mortgage on this property. In essence, let your tenants pay your way to a financially independent future.

I rate rental apartments as one of the best investments you can make.

Commercial Rentals

Commercial buildings range from small strip shopping areas or individual office buildings to major shopping centers. The management of the smaller buildings is relatively easy, and the tenants generally stay longer than do apartment tenants. My own experience with strip stores has been good, but the larger shopping centers never appealed to me because of the competition between major shopping areas. It is easy to lose a major tenant when the shopping trends shift to new or other parts of town.

Management of large properties of any nature can be very time-consuming and needs staff that know how to entice new tenants and how to keep the operational expenses at a level that supports a profit at the end of the year.

Unlike rental apartments, commercial rental facilities do not have the immediate exit into condominiums. Of course, there are condominium offices, and condominium warehouses, but generally retail rentals stay exactly that until the land becomes more valuable than the existing facilities.

Condo-Hotels

A condo-hotel can be several different types of hotel, or combination apartment hotel and condominium. Developers that "sell" condominium hotel units reach out to an investor who may frequently travel to the area and wants to have his own place to stay. The presumed advantage in buying a condo-hotel unit is that when the owner is not in town it can be rented out by the in-house management.

This can have real appeal, especially when the alternative kind of unit to buy might be a regular condominium apartment building, which, as is often the case, has restrictions on renting units to outsiders. Most condominium apartment home owners associations either outright prohibit rentals, or limit them to one a year and then require that the prospective tenants go through a rather elaborate screening process that all but eliminates the idea of renting the unit to a number of people for short periods of time.

A well-established condo-hotel has an upscale exit potential, which may make the condo-hotel a great investment. The exit would be to ultimately convert the condo-hotel into a timeshare or vacation club property. I will get to timeshares and vacation clubs shortly, but consider the kind of location where timeshare facilities are sold. To get a quick lesson in this, log on to RCI.com and search their locations. They are found all over the place, in almost every country of the world. But they are concentrated in the Sun Belt and where ever people holiday, ski, play golf (year round better), and vacation. The word "vacation" is important because this opens the timeshare doors, as well as the hotel and condo-hotel doors to people who visit major cities around the world, too.

The exit strategy works for the investor this way. The developer buys an existing hotel that is priced right because it needs a lot of tender loving care and upgrades. The developer now fixes up a couple model units to show what the fully renovated all suite hotel will look like. The investor also has negotiated with a flag name to put on the hotel that solidifies the idea that good times will be just around the corner for the hotel's new owners. Then the sales start and before you know it, the 400-unit hotel that is now a planned 200 all suite condo-hotel is off and running. The developer has pre-timeshared the property, by taking all the necessary legal steps to insure that any owner of one of the condo-hotel units can subdivide that unit into its true time-share time intervals, generally a one-week period of time. An essential ingredient of this would be an association with one of the major timeshare names. Resort Condo-miniums International (RCI, which is owned by Cendant Corporation, a powerhouse in the travel industry) and Interval International (II) are two of the major timeshare exchange networks. But there are others, and independent timeshare developers like Marriott, Hyatt, Hilton, and Disney, to name a few as well as Fairfield Communities (also owned by Cendant Corporation) all operate in-house exchanges to their devel-oped, managed or associated properties that other people or companies (like yours perhaps) have developed.

The plan and sales strategy for a project like this is for the developer to operate the condo-hotel as a hotel and in a few years begin to sell the weeks that owners are now asked to contribute to the sales effort. The original developer will, of course, take a healthy percentage from the sale as their cost of sale and profit. The owner of the unit (now weeks of timeshare intervals) will profit nicely as the prices of timeshares is often at the top of the market price per square foot.

This is a new concept that will likely revolutionize both the timeshare industry and the condo-hotel concept. To get into this business takes some deep pockets and ex-perience in one or more of the necessary management skills that go with the develop-ment, sales, and management of the end product. This kind of real estate investment is great, however, since millions of dollars are made in this industry. It would be a good choice if you were already in the hotel business and needed or wanted to find a prof-itable exit for your hotels.

Conversions

If you do not know it by now, then take note, one of the very best things you can do is to buy a property that is priced below the market and then to sell it well above that market. But there is a catch to this statement. You purchase a property that is below its market because of what it is . . . say a tired-looking motel, and you turn it into a different use, like a retirement home or an office building.

Economic conversions of any kind are born because the developer or investor has studied the local zoning ordinances and knows exactly what else is allowed on a site instead of what is currently there.

The ultimate management of the property, once developed, will depend on the type of conversion that results. The key to a conversion that might suit you as an investor will be what you are comfortable with, and how well you have picked the best new use. It would be a grave mistake to try to convert a property into a use other than what it currently is, simply because you were the world expert in another use, say, funeral homes, when there is no void in the marketplace for another funeral home. Equally, if you were the world expert in fast food joints, you might know better than to convert an old motel into a food court of fast food establishments 50 miles from town at the junction of two interstates in Nebraska. Or (I am not an expert in fast food joints) you could be a genius and on the next cover of *Money* magazine.

The key to success in conversions is knowledge of the immediate real estate market where you are investing. Tie that to an in-depth knowledge of the local zoning ordinances and you can start looking for properties that are not successful or profitable, because their use is outdated, no longer in vogue, or declining in condition. You can profit if you have found that the property is zoned for another use that will make you a ton of money.

Hotels and Motels

In his autobiography, Conrad Hilton (of the Hilton hotel fame) suggested that the idea of ownership of a hotel is one of the great afflictions of the wealthy. I believe that Conrad knew what he was talking about too because many wealthy people gravitate toward ownership of this kind of real estate. The interesting thing about ownership of a hotel is that most hotels employ many people. *So what?* You might ask. Well, if you owned one and wanted to manage it, you, your whole family, and their generations of family could count on a job. Of course, the new members of the family would have to start at the bottom, but then many happy millionaires had to follow that kind of route.

I personally like the idea of hotels as a route to wealth. I have already mentioned the condo-hotel concept, which is an exit from ownership of a hotel, but that can lead to timeshares and a continued management operation in a property that has none of your capital invested. Now that is a good way to exit a property. It is like having your cake and eating it to.

But, on the down side, hotel operations are wrought with management problems. Naturally, much of this will depend on the size of the property, and how your clientele is enticed to come to the property in the first place. But, if you are not willing to take a job at a hotel (or have a relative who owns one hire you), then skip this kind of property.

Industrial Buildings

As I write this, I am reminded that industrial property is often one of the scarcest zoning in any community. Development of these kinds of buildings is not difficult, if you have development experience, and they are often leased in advance of their construction. Industrial building leases are frequently triple net (NNN) which means the tenant pays everything associated with the maintenance, repair, upkeep, and all the expenses associated with the property such as taxes, insurance, casualty damage, plus a base rent. All the owner has to do is to cash the base rent check and pray the tenant does not go out of business.

However, any tenant can go out of business, or simply do a midnight checkout that you do not discover for a week or two. Because of this, industrial leases, since many are NNN leases, become a challenge since it is necessary to check, then double check the tenants' credit and past history of meeting their rental obligations in other facilities. There is some risk in renting to almost any tenant. U.S. post offices used to be the sweetheart of all leases, but now many post offices are small satellite facilities that often are either the prelude to a larger facility or are the downsize of such a facility. But no tenant can be considered as absolutely permanent, and as the lease starts to approach the final years, there is always the chance that the existing tenant will bail out of his or her lease by subleasing to a short-term tenant. Some long-term tenants just shut down and move out of the building because the building is so out of date that it costs them too much to maintain and it pays them to hand over the rent for the last couple of years and let the building become a dark box. "Dark box," by the way, is the term for a large building of any kind that could be industrial, warehouse, or a former Kmart or other kind of large retail store that has moved on to greener more productive pastures.

There is a high risk in some large buildings that have only a few tenants. If one or more does not renew their lease, or goes out of business, you can be left with space that is difficult to rent out. Tenant improvements can also be expensive in the rent up process. I do not recommend these kinds of buildings for the novice real estate investor. A larger variety of tenants can offer a landlord a better opportunity to rent if a tenant moves out.

Shopping Centers and Office Buildings

I have already mentioned shopping centers, but let's, for the moment, tie them to office buildings. I do this because the leases of each have a certain similarity that is beneficial to the investors. That is the CAM (Common Area Maintenance) provisions that are usually contained within those leases. This means that the tenants are responsible for all the common area maintenance costs in a pro rata relationship to their square footage to the total square footage of the property. If there is a million square feet of rentable area in the complex, and you are a tenant for 100,000 square feet, then you will have to pay, in addition to your rent, 10 percent of the actual CAM cost.

Think about this for a moment. If all your tenants are signed up on leases that say, "whatever it cost to own and operate this complex you pay your share" how wonderful your life is. That is, how wonderful it is until your Ferraris-R-Us tenant goes broke and leaves you with 200,000 square feet of empty space.

Shopping centers that reach mall size are truly big business. They have major staffs that deal with the constant upgrade of tenant make-up, and every few years go through the tenant build-out for new tenants moving in. One good approach to becoming an owner of a shopping center is to own the land under one. Commercial land leases can be found under many different types of real estate, including shopping centers. Because land is not a depreciable item, some investors would rather put their cash into the income part of the property and simply rent the rest. By owning the land, the owner is insulated from the changeover of tenants, which is the problem of the owner of the center who pays rent to the landowner.

But there is a problem of risk with large debt. When there are land leases, the lender who financed the original center or the new owner's acquisition may demand that the landowner subordinate the land to the mortgage. This act would put the land in the combination as a part of the security to the mortgage. This can be very risky, but if the risk is warranted and the return is attractive, then go for it.

Single-Family Homes

In the end, the largest investment that the average person will ever make is the purchase of his or her home. Buying a home is, most of the time, a grand step into the world of real estate and will turn out on the positive side. But that depends on many variables. Did the investor do his or her due diligence on where and how to buy the property? Did she finance it in such a way that it would not overburden her economic capabilities? And, perhaps most important, was that buyer ready to accept the responsibility of ownership of real estate in the first place.

Owning a home is like owning a boat, only the boat will take you fishing. Both homes and boats can be bottomless pits of expenses. Yard and pool maintenance, replacement of AC units, repair of roofs and plumbing, real estate taxes up the kazoo, and, well, the list goes on. Are you ready for that, or are you content to pay your monthly rent and let the landlord worry about the headaches of ownership. Oh . . . I almost forgot, in some parts of the United States, rising insurance and real estate taxes, are killing homeowners (and other property owners too).

Still, single-family homes can and do make sound investments when the circumstances are at their most favorable. This would be the case when there is high employment in the area that supports home ownership (and not just renters), and where there is a strong resale market of older homes. If you are in an area where new homes are selling like hotcakes, but older homes are not moving at all, then you have found an area where home prices are in the leveling-off stage. When that happens, people would rather own something new, than something old, or it could be that the older neighborhoods have become undesirable or less desirable due to many different circumstances. The most pronounced of those situations would be a rise in crime, infrastructure problems that force heavy traffic through the older residential areas, or unemployment that forces the owners of the older properties to remain there because they can not afford to move into newer properties.

If you avoid areas that meet the above description, purchasing a single-family home is a good long-term choice for people who can afford the home in the first place.

Tenant-in-Common Investments

There is a provision that came out of the IRS that is called IRC Section 1031. This is the section of the Internal Revenue Code that controls what real estate insiders call, "the tax free exchange." It is also simply called a 1031 exchange. It is a highly technical method where you can sell or exchange your investment property and reinvest in another investment property and not pay any capital gains tax on profit you make in the transaction. This code started out covering only exchanges. However, thanks to a transaction named for the person who did it, Mr. Starker, there is now a procedure that you can follow where you actually sell your property and still not pay the taxes. How? You put the proceeds into a special place where you cannot touch it yourself, and let the independent third party you hire reinvest in another property you have chosen.

This concept has created a great way to build equity without having it diluted by capital gains tax. But things have gotten better because now you can move the proceeds of a sale into a share in a much larger property that has been divided up between other investors like yourself. Not totally unlike a share of a Real Estate Investment Trust (REIT) that is sold like stock, the Tenant-in-Common share (TIC) is sold by stockbrokers or properly licensed realtors as a qualified reinvestment for any 1031 treatment property.

From the real estate investor point of view, it is best to be on the formation side of this kind of property. By this I mean, go out and form your own TIC. Other investors, who are struggling with the IRC 1031 short time table to meet the deadline on finding a replacement property, will come to you so that they can save not having to pay the capital gains tax on their sale.

Because TIC investments are highly regulated by the IRS with lots of special rules to be followed, it would be essential that you study this aspect in depth before making a move in that field.

Timeshares

These are also called interval ownership, vacation clubs, and so on. They come in a variety forms of ownership.

Warranty Deed: There is the outright warranty deed that a buyer gets when he purchases title to a specific time of the year. Week 12 is generally the week that begins on the 12th Friday or Saturday of the year. But this is not etched into stone, so you need to make sure exactly what period of the year your week begins and how that changes every year.

Floating Time: This is a week of time, but it varies every year. Each timeshare that has floating time may have a different method of assigning the week each year, and some of the methods are designed by the same people who write the IRS codes (I am convinced of this, but have no proof of that fact).

Points Systems: These are relatively new and seem to be the future for timeshare as well as vacation clubs. The investors buying the unit do not actually get a unit; what they get is a block of points that can be used to access units. Many of the timeshare developers who started selling with the warranty deed system are converting into the points format. Fairfield Resorts, which I introduced to you earlier in this chapter, is moving toward points, and their points are much like airline miles and can be used to purchase or "rent" other timeshare units in a large system. At the same time these points can be used to "buy" a cruise, rent a hotel room or car, and so on. There are limitations to the duration of the points, so unlike airline miles that can stay in our account for a long time, Fairfield's points either get used for an immediate rental or an exchange for a rental of a fixed week somewhere in the system. However, like just about everything in the timeshare, marketing is going through constant modification and improvement, so this system is likely to continue to improve its value to its investors.

Fractional Ownership: This is a division of ownership in the same timeshare unit that is down the street, but instead of being broken into one week the interval can be anything from a month to a quarter of a year. Quarter-shares identify the three-month ownership period. To make this a bit more interesting, this three-month period might not be a continuous three months and might even shift around during succeeding years.

Vacation Clubs: These are an even newer vacation program that may include mansions, deluxe condominiums in exotic places, or just that one beautiful home overlooking the sunsets in a remote Greek island. Owners of these clubs pay big bucks, often over a $100,000, to have a chance at one of these locations each year for a period of time.

All owners in all the other forms mentioned pay the initial purchase and pay annual fees. These annual fees cover membership in the organization, maintenance costs (much like the CAM charges in a commercial rental), and management, as well as their share of real estate taxes, which is often quoted separately from the annual maintenance charge.

Okay, so this is big business, and the investors who are in this kind of business are often first in the marketing side of the operation, and the development side by default. It is not something that is easy to get into unless you are already a hotel owner who wants to go through the easier steps of converting to a condo-hotel first and then ease into the timeshare business.

Vacant Land

There are two ways to buy vacant land and to profit handsomely. The first is to have an immediate use for the land. In this, you need the land as the base for something else. That restaurant that you know will be a big money maker, or the used car lot you want to own and operate, or whatever it is that you need a location for *now*.

The "now" part of this equation is important because any real estate investor who is a developer and operator is willing to pay more for that immediate use. So, this first vacant landowner wants to buy only if the land is ready to be used for what he wants, or if the seller will warrant that the approvals can be obtained for that use. If there is no ultimate approval, then the deal does not continue and the investor moves to his second choice. There is that word "approval" again. If you were the seller in this instance, your sale might fall flat on its face because some Planning Official voted no, and the board turned the use down.

The second way to profit from vacant land is to purchase land that is in the fairly immediate path of progress and to go through an approval process that will convert that land to a higher economic use. You do this even if you have no intention of following through with that use yourself.

It is generally not difficult to see where growth is coming from and the direction the growth is headed. You then pick a spot that you may project to be three to five years distant from that growth. The truly smart insider will then contract to purchase a tract of land and proceed to improve the use of that land. By "improve the use" I do not mean that the investor will build something there. That might come later on, but for now the investor wants to create new value by adding potential to the land.

If the property is presently zoned agricultural land that has limited residential use, say one home for every 20 acres of area, the land supports a use with limited economic potential. However, if the investor has done her homework properly she may realize that the local government will allow the land to be rezoned to permit two or three (or more) residential homes per acre. Add the possibility of a site for a shopping center and other commercial uses; now the land jumps up in value the moment the approval is in hand. However, if an investor blindly believes that such approvals are simply obtained and purchased in the path of progress, but without hope of getting approvals, that investor may have made a costly mistake.

So, the best way to speculate in land is to know ahead of time what the local authorities will permit, be familiar with the building codes and other ordinances that may limit the use (even though the zoning says it is an approval use), and then move forward.

It is a good idea to have some interim use for large tracts of land that you may have to sit on for a number of years, even after you have improved the economic use of this property. These uses can help with the expenses to carry the property and at the same time provide extra income.

In areas of the country that have special real estate tax rates for agricultural land uses, you should check out the opportunity to get an exemption from the regular tax rate by finding out exactly what you need to do to obtain those exemptions. In Florida, for example, the ad valorem tax rate goes way down for any approved agricultural use. Get a copy of that list, as you will be surprised what is approved. It might be that a landscape-growing field is approved just like a U-Pick-It corn or strawberry field, or perhaps leasing the land to a farmer to graze his cows, horses, sheep, or llamas puts that land into agricultural use.

What Can Get Investors into Trouble

Now that we have reviewed the kinds of property you can chose from and the pros and cons of those properties I would like to call attention to some of the individual investor's traits that can get you, as an investor, into trouble. I think you will quickly see that the negative traits will appear to be very obvious, but let me caution you, it is far more obvious when they are pointed out to you than when you see them in reality. The more important ones are these:

The Green Grass Syndrome

Blind as a Bat

The Big G Word

Over the Leverage Cliff

The Mouth Trap

Fear Itself

The Green Grass Syndrome

You have heard the saying "The grass always looks greener on the other side of the fence." Well, when it comes to real estate, this is one of the most dangerous of all investor pitfalls.

Virtually every investor is going to fall for this one at least once. It can be the beautiful sunset over the Pacific Ocean that makes the investor fall in love with the view from that Acapulco penthouse that is for sale, or the shear beauty of the Red Rocks of Sedona, Arizona, or the tranquil beauty of Bermuda.

It might also be the price difference. "My goodness, it is so inexpensive to live in Santiago de Chile." But then, jobs also pay less.

Be wary of anything new that suddenly looks like a great deal.

Blind as a Bat

"I can't see the trees because of the forest," the would-be real estate investor was saying. What he meant was the single tree that he should purchase is lost in the maze of properties that all look the same. The ability to see which properties will present an opportunity takes some practice and a lot of learning and effort. It is not as simple as falling off a log, although that is surely what will happen if the investor falls into the green grass pitfall.

Fall back on the new three most important words about real estate: "Location, Use, Approval" and then think of the things that make them pertinent to your investment needs. It is critical to stay focused on this because if you start out looking for the best buy in a site to build and sell condominiums, and end up buying a great site to build single-family homes at a much lower density, then you have made a mistake as far as your original goals were considered.

Having specific criteria that you need to match up with your ultimate investment property is important, so be sure to check with the local officials (planning, zoning, and building departments as well as the utility companies) to ascertain exactly what you will need to accomplish what you want.

The Big G Word

The word is "Greed," and it is that wolf that will eventually bite you unless you are very careful. Its bite may not kill you, but it sure can kill a real estate transaction. It generally rears its head in the middle of negotiations, and it can affect one or both parties of the transaction. Sellers suddenly want more out of the deal, or buyers want to keep more in their pocket and pay less. Whatever the situation, the deal is likely headed for the trash heap unless the parties can get back on track.

That track is the attainment of the original goals that were the catalyst to the negotiation process in the first place.

Sellers want to sell, or can be enticed to sell when that process takes them closer to a predetermined goal. It is important, if you are a seller or become one that you have thought out what you are going to do with the proceeds of the sale. This is important for many reasons, not just the avoidance of the G word. Planning for your financial future requires that you do this, otherwise you may miss one or more IRS loopholes that can save you on capital gains taxes. But it is absolutely essential that you enter the negotiation process with some end use in sight.

Buyers need to stay focused to those long-term or end-use goals, for the obvious reason that if they don't, then they have let emotion or green grass or the lack of due diligence get into their way.

Staying focused to your goals and having goals that can be visualized and measured, by a timetable are the best key to your ultimate success.

Over the Leverage Cliff

There are times when extreme leverage is okay. For example, assume all you can afford is $1,000 a month in rent. On top of that, you do not have enough cash for a down payment on a home or condominium. Now it is okay for you to purchase, even if you finance 100 percent of the purchase price, if you do not increase your annual cost of that ownership at more than $12,000 plus the income tax you might otherwise have paid. It was necessary to throw that income tax thing into this example because when you rent you do not get any tax breaks at all. However, when you own and pay a mortgage, all the interest you pay on the mortgage may be deductible, subject to some limits if the mortgage amount is greater than the value of the property. That and other tax deductions from real estate ownership ease the drain on your pocketbook and should be taken into account in any direct comparison, such as rent versus ownership.

Real estate investors who are looking to max out equity buildup may anticipate that if they start with little or no equity, then any buildup at all will be at a fantastic rate. The idea works mathematically, but in real life the key to buildup is to first be able to cover the expenses and debt service of the investment. Failure to do that means that the investor is pouring capital into the property just to meet expenses (and likely debt service). This is a frequently occurring event, which may have been predictable from a more conservative proforma of the investment's potential.

The Mouth Trap

The investor, buyer, or seller sometimes speaks too quickly and says too much too soon, and the result is a blown deal. As a realtor, and often a third-party observer of negotiations, I am never surprised at how quickly a deal can deteriorate because of what is said. The interesting thing about this is that it is usually the seller that makes this mistake.

Sellers are prone to exaggerate income or potential of the property they are selling and to downplay expenses and drawbacks (if any exist, and they usually do). Of all the potential statements that a seller can utter, the truth may be the more elusive of all. Untruths can occur when a salesperson doesn't want to appear to be stupid or ignorant, so instead of saying, "I don't know the square footage of this building, but I will find out for you," he might say, "It is 200,000 square feet." Sometimes the truth is hidden by the big lie as soon as the Big Mouth opens up, and the lie becomes evident.

Unfortunately, there is another party or two that can also be caught by the Big Mouth situation. The real estate agent. To pretend that salesmen and saleswomen of any marketing program never exaggerate or outright lie would be to avoid reality. It happens, and as a long time commercial realtor, I can say that much of my career has been doing all I could to make sure that my agents never fell into the Big Mouth pit. Oh, but the G word often is a very attractive motivator.

The greatest rule any investor should follow is to never believe anything you hear unless you have verified it yourself or through your investment team in which you have absolute trust and confidence.

Fear Itself

Fear to move forward stops many investors dead in their tracks. Now, there is nothing wrong with fear as long as it causes investors to second guess their own ability. Double-checking can be part of the cure to overcoming fear, but it is critical for the investor to be cautious about who is giving what advice. People who will profit from your decision to move forward or, for that matter, to withdraw, may not be in a position to give you the kind of advise that you need.

The opposite of a decision not to move forward, simply because of the fear of failing, would be the decision to move forward because of overconfidence. Each factor can be debilitating.

The interesting thing about this is that many real estate investors have made millions of dollars simply by acting out of some blind good luck when they were at the right place at the right time and said, "Let's go for it".

Now Build a Comfort Zone Investment Strategy

A comfort zone is the geographic area in which you look for your investments. It will be a small part of town, in the first stages of investing. As you grow increasingly knowledgable of that area, you can begin to expand it. However, there is no need to expand just for expansion's sake. I know many real estate investors who have bought and sold property within a few blocks of where they live. Some condominium dwellers buy and sell in the same complex where they live and do very well in that confined area. Real estate is a unique item. It allows very narrow direct comparison between areas of the country, even areas of the same town. Because of this, it is relatively easy for all investors to become expert in what is going on within their own comfort zone.

Key Factors You Need to Look For in Your Comfort Zone

The goal for development of an effective comfort zone is to define a geographic area that is confined within the same governing authority. By this, I mean your initial comfort zone should be within the same city, so that you do not have to deal with conflicting governmental departments. This becomes critical when learning the essentials of zoning and building codes and regulations. These are two items that can vary greatly between cities, even neighboring cities.

Local politics may also be in conflict between neighboring cities. One can be pro development, the other against development. When you have a potential choice between different cities, go with the city that has a pro development attitude.

Once you have defined the kind of property you want to buy, then look around the overall area of authority to see which part of this city you want to concentrate on first. Make sure that you choose a large enough area to give you a variety of the property of the category you have selected. Not all of this property will be for sale, so you need to have enough to chose from to form an investment base. If rental apartments not larger than 50 units are your initial choice, as an example, you need at least 50 such properties in the area to give you sufficient real estate to work with. Lower-priced properties, such as single-family homes, or condominiums, require a larger concentration of selected properties so the zone will need to be expanded.

The plan to develop your comfort zone requires you to learn everything you can about the elements that cause value to rise and fall. But you must also learn the market trends, because they will lead you to the best areas where the best opportunities will be found.

Map out this comfort zone and establish the current status quo. That is, what is the situation as it now exists. From this you can set a point where things will go either up or down in value and or growth. Take a look at the following checklists as you get ready to invest in real estate.

The Nine Key Elements That Control the Value of Your Comfort Zone

1. Road works and changes

2. Infrastructure changes

3. Building rules and regulations change

4. Zoning ordinance changes

5. Future real estate developments in the works

6. Utility changes being planned

7. Potential increases or decreases of local employment

8. Local Government's attitude toward development

9. Natural barriers that funnel growth pattern

Where You Find Your Comfort Zone Data

Agendas of city meetings

Building departments

City commission meetings

County commission meetings

Departments of transportation

DRC meetings

Economic development boards

Fire department

Local news media

Local utility companies

Major employers in the area

Planning departments

Planning meetings

School boards

Tax assessor's office

Zoning departments

CHAPTER 4

How Financing Affects Cash Flow and Equity Buildup

The goal of this chapter is:

To Open Your Eyes to the Effects of Debt

Debt is using other people's money. It is the spice of life for the real estate investor because it enables the investor with cash to divide that cash between several different properties. Best of all, if the investor does not have cash, debt brings other people's cash to the table and allows the investor to own real estate. No matter if the goal is cash flow or equity buildup, the goal is to let the tenants or revenue from the property pay off the debt. In Chapter One, I discussed some of the elements of debt and how to calculate mortgage payments. This chapter will expand your knowledge of how to work through problems to obtain the maximum benefits from the debt you create.

Terms and Concepts You Need to Know

Presumed Value

Value Added

Delayed Payments

Hard Costs and Soft Costs

Construction Draws

Cost to Carry the Debt

Interest Only, Deficit Interest, Fixed Interest, and Variable Interest

Amortized Principal, Fixed Principal Reduction, Variable Principal, and Balloon
    Payments

Options

Institutional Lenders

Seller-Held Mortgages

Exchanges—1031 and Otherwise

Sweat Equity

Review each in detail.

Presumed Value

When an investor makes a presentation to a prospective lender, it is reasonable that the investor will state a presumed value of the property, which will become the security to the mortgage. The idea of a presumed value can get a bit muddled when the investor does not own or even have a contract to purchase that property yet, especially if the "presumed value" is higher than the purchase price asked by the seller.

Nonetheless, all presentations that are made with the anticipated future value of a property deal with this concept of presumed value. The validity of this format, from the lender's point of view will depend on the success of the investor to present the case in such a way that the ultimate loan to value ratio will be within the comfort zone of that lender.

Take for example an investor who wants to purchase a run-down restaurant that has been closed for several years. It occupies a prime corner of two highly trafficked local streets, which connect several schools and hospitals with other general commercial enterprises. But as a viable restaurant it failed because it did not have sufficient parking for a sit-down restaurant.

This investor wants to put a copy of his very successful restaurant on the other side of town that is a take-out restaurant with only a small, bar-type seating area for wine and tapas while the patrons wait for their take-out food. Due to the limited number of patrons able to sit in this waiting area, the small allotment of parking was not a drawback.

This investor can project a future value of this "failed restaurant" based on the success of his other restaurant. By making a projection along this basis, and being conservative as to the build-up time for the business, a realistic presumed value can be projected.

Proformas, which are a projected view of the income and expenses of a new or converted property, also result in a presumed value based on anticipated cash flow. This kind of value differs from a value that is derived from a more formal appraisal that takes into account comparative analysis of similar properties, recent sales of similar properties, and a cost to reproduce approach.

Value Added

Sometimes the value of a property can be increased by a restructure of the ownership, or modification of its use that may not even be visible. This is a very subtle event and can occur almost overnight. The term "value added" was invented by accounting firms that deal with Real Estate Investment Trusts (REITs), and has since expanded into the vocabulary of other types of real estate ownership. In the case of REITs, they are sometimes formed by the former owners of the real estate that they initially own. A shopping center owner, such as Simon DeBartolo Inc., decided to take their centers and instead of being a privately held company, they would become a publicly held Real Estate Investment Trust. The move from private to public did not change the real estate at all, not one penny of new revenue was being produced. Yet the total value of the stock being traded in the open public arena was greater than the total value of the real estate the day before the change. REIT accountants and founders argue that there was indeed value added because the liquidity of the stock was greater.

This is, of course a debatable matter, since the value of stock does not just go up; it can, and does quite frequently, go down.

Delayed Payments

In the previous chapters I introduced several mortgage situations that had payment schedules that had periods of time when payments were withheld. This can occur in a number of ways, and the result is generally to allow the buyer of a property time to ease into the property without having heavy, or any, debt service. The concept of delayed payments also is applied to lease payments, especially when the tenant is making expensive tenant improvements to remodel or build-out the facilities.

In negotiations, property owners or sellers of property often prefer to offer or agree to a request for such a method of payment rather than an outright reduction of the principal amount of a mortgage or the base rent portion of a lease. The reason for this is that when the payments on a mortgage commence the interest continues on the larger amount of the principal owned, and with leases annual cost of living increases are applied to a larger original base rent instead of a reduced amount.

For example, if the seller was to hold a $500,000 mortgage that called for $5,000 a month in payments (over 15 years at 8 percent interest), and the buyer insists on relief from any mortgage payments for the first six months. The end result of this relief to the buyer will be that the cash flow will reflect an increase at the end of the year by this

$30,000 not paid on the debt. Had the seller simply reduced the price by $30,000, it would have had to come off the down payment for it to have the same impact. By reducing the mortgage principal by that same amount, ergo a mortgage of $470,000 the monthly payments would have dropped to approximately $4,712 and would not have achieved the desired results.

To change the perspective of this, assume that the property in question was negotiated to an overall price of $700,000 and the buyer had offered to exchange a vacant lot clearly worth $230,000, and the seller had agreed to that, plus to hold a first mortgage for $470,000. The buyer goes through due diligence and comes back to renegotiate the deal. "I'll close tomorrow," the buyer begins, "but you have to help me out. Give me a moratorium of six months, and we can make the mortgage amount $500,000." You should see now that this format has certain advantages to both parties (assuming the seller wants the lot and doesn't need the ready cash from the payments). Clearly the buyer benefits because the buyer's overall payment is the same.

Tenants are often enticed to rent a vacant apartment or commercial space because the landlord agrees to "free rent" which is, of course, really a delay in rent so that the tenant can get moved in and fix the space or apartment to suit its needs.

Hard Costs and Soft Costs

The hard cost of real estate generally applies to acquisition, and material and labor of any new construction. Soft costs generally relate to all the other costs except for interest related to any debt tied to the deal. For example, if you purchased a vacant site for $100,000 and hired a general contractor to build an office building, your hard cost would be the $100,000 and the contractor's material and labor. Your soft cost would be everything else. Your total cost would be any expenses incurred to borrow money (if you borrowed any) to be applied to this transaction. In this example, the contractor would likely charge you a percentage of the material and labor as the contractor's soft cost and call it "overhead and profit."

Construction Draws

When a lender, such as a local commercial bank, provides a development or construction loan, the loan is set up in such a way that it will be funded slowly over the life of the construction. For example, First Bank of Chicago agrees to finance the development of a motel in Springfield. Assume the total amount of the loan will be $3,000,000. The bank will agree to pay to the borrower this amount in "construction draws" as the development progresses. The amount of draws will vary, and generally follow a customary pattern for the stages of the development. The final draw will not come until the project is completed and all inspections by the necessary building officials and certificate of occupancy have been given, allowing occupancy of the building.

Cost to Carry the Debt

As the construction loan is paid out to the borrower, this loan begins to earn interest to the lender. One of the costs of any project, then, must also include the payment of this interest to the lender. This cost is sometimes included in the soft costs of the project, but should be shown as a separate item, since it is not a cost of the project, but a cost of borrowing money for that project. In any event, be sure that you anticipate that there is a cost to carry debt somewhere in the proforma of a project or you may fall short in the middle of development. If you have ever seen a construction site become a ghost site, with no one visible working there for months, this could well be an example of a faulty proforma.

Interest Only, Deficit Interest, Fixed Interest, and Variable Interest

All of these have been mentioned already in various examples, but take another look at how these can be used in creative contract negotiations.

Interest Only and Deficit Interest: If there are to be any payments on the mortgage at all, interest only will allow the borrower the greatest cash flow possible. Of course, the actual interest paid can be *deficit interest* where only a portion of the interest due is paid and the amount lacking is added to the principal owed. This is a unique way to structure a mortgage and yet is rarely used, despite certain benefits to the lender. Take a look at the following example.

Roland is a seller who is highly motivated to get rid of a management problem in the form of a rental apartment building. Along comes Phil who is a carpenter with the time and knowledge to fix up the place and to deal with its poor tenant structure. Roland wants to set up two college funds for his two grandchildren, so he agrees to take $40,000 cash down, let the carpenter assume the existing first mortgage in the amount of $200,000 and hold a $60,000 second mortgage. The mortgage is set at 8 percent interest only with only 1 percent of the outstanding balance being paid, while 7 percent goes back as additional principal owned. Roland then sets up two college funds at his local bank and has the trust officer handle the transaction. The 1 percent interest actually paid by Phil goes to the trust officer to cover collection costs and administration of the trust. The second mortgage is to balloon in 12 years and the funds paid into each of the two college funds equally. At the end of the 12 years (if not paid off earlier) each of these two college funds would now have $67,565 safely awaiting payment to some college.

Fixed Interest: This is the term used for a mortgage where the interest, or contract rate charged on the principal owned remains fixed during the term of the loan, or during a specific period of the loan. Do not assume that just because the term "fixed" is used that it means for the entire length of the loan. While it may indeed mean that, it might also be described in fine (usually blue ink on light blue paper) as "fixed for the first five years of the loan.

Variable Interest: This is an interest rate that is subject to changes over the life of the loan. There are many different methods of adjusting these rates, as are all terms of a mortgage, are negotiable and will vary between lenders. The key with these variable rates is that any borrower should learn to protect itself by spelling out the method of variation, the maximum increase that the lender can make at any given time, and/or over the life of the loan. It would be beneficial to have the lender provide you with a detailed example of the usual and maximum changes that could occur.

Amortized Principal, Fixed Principal Reduction, Variable Principal, and Balloon Payments

Amortized principal is the gradual reduction of the outstanding principal owed on the loan. In the case where interest payments are only partially paid or not paid at all and those amounts are added to the principal outstanding, there would not be any principal amortization. This event would cause the principal owed to vary.

The gradual payments may be fixed amounts, such as the following mortgage. Assume the investor borrows $100,000 and agrees to repay the principal over 20 years at $5,000 principal per year, at the end of the year, together with 8 percent interest on the principal amount outstanding. In this loan there would be a $13,000 total payment made up of a $5,000 principal and an $8,000 (.08 × $100,000) interest payment. At the end of the second year, the payment would be $12,300 made up of $5,000 principal and $7,600 interest (.08 × 95,000). Each year the principal payment will remain the same, whereas the interest is charged on the declining principal outstanding so it is reduced by $400 each year until the final payment of $5,400, which would be made up of $5,000 principal and $400 interest (.08 × 5,000). See the first five years of this mortgage that follows:

Fixed Principal Annual Payment First Five Years

Amount of Principal			
Owed at Start of Year	Paid at end of Year	Interest Paid (8%)	Total Payment
$100,000	$5,000	$8,000	$13,000
95,000	5,000	7,600	12,600

90,000	5,000	7,200	12,200
85,000	5,000	6,800	11,800
80,000	5,000	64,00	11,400

Variable Principal: Variable principal can be a principal amount that increases, as I have described earlier, or it can be a payment during the term of the loan that varies. For example, a loan may be set up to have a series of principal payments made that occur at set or different times of the life of the loan at different amounts. These payments are called balloon payments. In the following example, I have combined several of the principal payment methods already discussed so that you can see how creative you can be.

An investor negotiates with a seller to hold a second mortgage in the amount of $200,000 at 8 percent interest with payments over five years. The loan has no payments at all during the first year, so there would be 8 percent interest added to the principal at the end of that first year. At the end of the second year, the investor pays interest due plus $25,000 of principal. At the end of the third year, there is only interest paid. At the end of the fourth year $80,000 of principal plus interest is paid.

Mortgage Where Principal and Interest Payments Vary

Amount of Principal

	Owed at Start of Year	*Paid at End of Year*	*Interest Paid (8%)*	*Total Payment*
1.	$200,000	0		
2.	216,000	$25,000	$17,280	$42,280
3.	191,000	0	15,280	15,280
4.	191,000	80,000	0	80,000
5.	125,280	125,280	10,022.40	$135,302.40

Options

Options are one of the greatest tools a real estate investor has in his bag of techniques. What makes them so useful is they enable an investor to tie up a property without having to purchase it (yet, if ever). This is a pre-closing technique that gives the buyer time to make inspections, get approvals that might be needed, but most important of all, it closes out other buyers, puts this investor in control of the property and buys time for the investor to make that ultimate decision: Should I buy or not.

Buy the Investor Cheap Time: Most contract options are really free time, because the buyer may insist that the option money will be lost only if the buyer does not exercise the option. In essence, suppose you give a seller of a $800,000 commercial site you want to purchase $25,000 for a six-month option. The seller agrees to let you use this period of time to make studies of the seller's property. If you end up buying the property, the seller agrees to count that $25,000 as part of the agreed to purchase price. Most sellers will agree to this kind of arrangement if they are motivated to sell, especially when you point out that if you walk from the deal they get to keep the money. But even if the seller is hard-nosed about that option money and insists that you lose it all, (or part of it), you have tied up the $800,000 property for only $25,000. The real bonus to you is if you were going to put up a building on this site, you now have a free period of time to get approvals for building plans and can start construction the day you close. Keep this in mind. When you know you are going to buy, and have a lag time between when you need to tie up the property and begin to use it, always seek an option of one form or another.

In other forms of options, the word *option* never shows up anywhere. These are contracted periods of time to make studies, and obtain permits and approvals. Land developers, for example, would not think of contracting land that they needed to build on without obtaining these approvals before closing on the site. This was not always the case, though. There was a time, not so distant ago, when getting approvals was a snap. Cities and governmental planners were easy to deal with, and development moved at a swift pace for most of the country. But things are gravely changed in that department, and sellers have, for the most part, become aware that long delays can occur for even simple plan approvals and are growing more acquainted with the needs of developers.

Close Out the Competition: One of the very best advantages that options give the investor is they close out the competition. This works wonders, and it doesn't matter if it is an actual "paid for" option, or a free option gained through the need to inspect or obtain approvals, or through whatever the provision in the contract enables the investor to be in control of the property without having to purchase it.

Too many investors want to spend time analyzing a property literally to death. By this I mean that by the time they have thought it through, which generally means got up the courage to make an offer, the property is dead, for them at least. Some other investors, who liked the property well enough to want to spend both time and money to see if it would work for them, knew that if they didn't tie-up the property it would be gone. Literally by the next day sometimes.

As a commercial real estate broker, I have encouraged my clients to act now and think it through once they were in control of the situation. If you think your real estate broker is pushing you to make a deal, that could be the case, but take this advice from a broker who is also an investor. Control is the name of the game. Talking about doing something without action will only get you the back seat, most of the time.

Institutional Lenders

The real estate market is an ocean full of waves. There are peaks and valleys, and if you pay attention long enough, some areas will be calm while others, perhaps a bit farther out from shore, will be rough as a tempest, and then the tide changes. The peaks and valleys and even the calm places are like the real estate market. And the tides ebb and flow, only on a far more predictable pattern than does real estate. The real estate lenders function best when they maintain a tight reign on the way the real estate market flows. Lenders depend on borrowers needing their funds, and borrowers need lenders willing and able to extend credit.

But both lenders and borrowers need to maintain a close relationship with each other. The successful borrowers work the money market by cultivating sources of funds that work with them. Those borrowers or investors know what any specific lender likes to loan on most, and so they know who to go to first if their proposed project fits that lender's criteria of a preferred loan.

But investors need to understand that institutional lenders do not loan their own money. They use other people's money just as the real estate investor does, only the institutional lenders have the biggest advantage of any player in the market because they get to go directly to that beautiful vault of money, the Federal Reserve if they need refills of cash to lend out.

Savings and loan institutions, for example, make loans, then package them into bundles or portfolios of loans and sell those loans to insurance companies and other banks. The local S&L may even service those loans at a small fee, and they earn praise from the insurance companies and other banks who buy bundles and portfolios that never have a bad loan in them.

So, the biggest worry of all loan officers is making a loan that goes sour. For this reason they look to the borrower almost as much (and in some cases even more so) than the real estate itself. As a real estate investor, you need to cultivate your reputation for doing what you say you will do, and doing it on time.

Seller-Held Mortgages

Sellers are the most motivated lenders of them all. That is, when they are motivated to sell. It is necessary, at times, to educate sellers to the benefits of helping a buyer purchase their property by holding a mortgage on the property they want to sell. There have been cycles in the real estate market when certain categories of real estate have been very difficult to sell. Now read my lips. Almost every category of real estate has been on that list of "difficult to sell" property at one time or another. And it is highly likely that they will be again at some time in your investment career.

Therefore, it is important that you learn the techniques that help buyers and sellers reach their most urgent goal. To sell a property that is a problem for them (at that time) or to purchase a property that will take them closer to another goal. Of all the techniques that work wonders in a calm (or slow) real estate market, it is those that allow buyers to get sellers to hold all or part of the transaction in the form of a mortgage or some other kind of debt.

In my book *Investing in Real Estate with Other People's Money*, I go into many different techniques in great detail. It is cram-packed with examples and techniques that every real estate investor, lender, and advisor should know of, and be able to use when they fit the situation.

It is critical that you approach every transaction, whether it be a purchase or a sale, by having a clear focus on what your goal is that the deal will achieve. With that in mind, it is far easier to either make the transaction work or to stop wasting time and to move on to another property or another buyer. But by having your goals clearly connected to what you are doing, you will look for the transaction that continually moves you in the direction of your goals.

Like having a life goal to be an airline pilot, or a racecar driver, or some other task that takes time, practice and devotion to reach, having an investment goal may also require interim steps that will move you toward the final goal.

Learn to be creative with your thought process and never be afraid to ask sellers if they will help you buy their property. You might be surprised that they really do want you to buy it and will be glad to help you.

Exchanges—1031 and Otherwise

The IRS approved Section 1031 is one of the greatest loopholes available to real estate investors. In my John Wiley & Sons book *The Tax-Free Exchange Loophole* published in 2005, I go into great detail discussing how this program works, what you have to do to qualify, and how to avoid problems that could cancel your right to use 1031 treatment to avoid paying capital gains tax. So, unless you have a copy of that book, you need a short course on how this code can help you keep 100 percent of your capital gains profits without ever having to pay tax on them.

First let me say that anything that comes from the IRS will be complicated, often vague, sometimes illogical, but always hard to grasp. Nonetheless here is a brief introduction to this section of the tax code as it relates to real estate.

The IRC (Internal Revenue Code) Section 1031: The code states that if you have a capital gain in the exchange or sale of an investment property, and you choose to follow the rules and regulations of Section 1031 you can effectively avoid paying any of the capital gains tax that may otherwise apply to that gain. There are several key words here that you need to understand how they come into play. The first is "investment property"; keep in mind that we are talking about real estate and not other kinds of property that are also governed by this section (such as the sale of business equipment). To qualify under Section 1031 treatment, the property you give up or relinquish (by exchange or sale) must be a property that you held as an investment. This will exclude your home (unless you have moved out and have turned it into a rental property), but will include almost any other kind of real estate as long as the intention of ownership was to hold it as an investment. So, if you purchased a vacant lot with the intention of building a home, you might have a hard time convincing the IRS agent during your audit, that the lot was really an investment.

Okay, investment real estate can be anything outside of your home or intended home. That means a condo or home that you have owned and rented out, an office building, or a shopping center—anything but what you use or intend to use as your residence.

When you exchange or sell this investment property, for the transaction to qualify for 1031 treatment you must replace the relinquished property with another "like kind" property. This term "like kind" is the problem child with 1031 transactions because people, even lawyers I know, tend to believe that means if you exchange or sell an office building you have to replace it with another office building. This is not the case at all. "Like kind" is in the wording because this code does apply to other types of investment property and in the case of real estate all you have to do is have another real estate type of investment. An office building for factory equipment would not qualify, just as a valuable stamp exchanged for factory equipment or an office building would not qualify.

Now things start to look easier, if you have a shopping center that you have owned for 30 years and had built it on a vacant lot you had purchased ten years before that, you could be sitting on a substantial increase in value of real estate, which you have depreciated down to the original cost of the land. I have brokered transactions of situations like this and that $10,000,000 shopping center could have a book value (called basis in tax lingo) of less than $200,000. How so?

1. The lot was purchased for $200,000 in 1966. During the first 10 years of ownership, the property was first rented to a U-Pick It farmer to give it an agricultural tax exemption, which lowered the property taxes (ad valorem) to a very low rate.

2. Ten years later, a major supermarket came along and asked the owners if they would build them a supermarket on the site. The owners did exactly that, along with 120,000 square feet of shops and other retail enterprises, including a Burger King restaurant.

3. The city to the north and the city to the south grew together, and this center was smack-dab in the middle of everything.

4. Over the next 30 years, the accountants for the owners depreciated all the improvements right down to zero. As the land could not be depreciated, the basis of the property, for tax purposes, was the original $200,000 in value.

5. Along comes a developer who wants to knock everything down to build a new more compact center and several hundred condominiums. This developer

offers the owners of the center $15,000,000. The capital gain is the $15,000,000 less the basis of $200,000 or $14,800,000 of gain. If the owner sells and pockets the cash, there will be a tax due of at least 15 percent based on the tax rates for that year. This would mean a capital gains tax of $2,220,000 would be due to the IRS.

However, because the seller knew about Section 1031, he had prepared himself and the transaction so that it would qualify. The investor had two different routes he could follow to avoid the tax.

1. He could enter into a qualified exchange for a replacement property. All the property has to be is an investment property of a real estate nature. And the value of the property would have to be equal or greater than that of the property he had relinquished. Or,

2. He could take the cash from the sale, and make sure it was delivered to a "facilitator" who would hold onto the money while the investor found a replacement property, which that money could then purchase for him. Again, the property would have to be of equal or greater to the relinquished property.

There are some complicated rules about the 1031, which make it cumbersome at times, and some investors start out trying to do a 1031 sale only to discover that finding a replacement property is not so easy, and even if one is found, getting the deal closed on time can be very difficult.

On time? That's right, as the code is presently written there is a time line that must be followed, or the attempt to avoid the capital gains tax will be ruled invalid. Here is how the time line works. There is a period of 180 days between the date the investor passes title of his sold property in which to take title of the new property that will replace the old one. Sometimes, there may actually be several properties needed to make up the value of the one sold, adding a bit more complication to the deal if one or more of those properties ends up being impossible to close on in time. But in general, the 180-day rule should be okay, but within that 180 days the very first 45 days (of the 180 days) is the maximum time the investor has to find and identify the replacement property or properties. More than one property can be identified of course, but the safe limit is three properties. Remember, they do not have to be identified until the forty-fifth day after delivery of title on the relinquished property.

Where the problems come in is that investors may not know if the sale of their own property is actually going to close until the day it does close. Buyers that have "out clauses" that allow them to walk way from the deal, sometimes use those provisions because they could not get financing, or approval for the new shopping center and condominiums they wanted to build or because they simply have changed their mind about buying.

Because of this kind of circumstance, and the lax attitude some sellers have about finding a replacement property, it is not unusual for a seller suddenly in need of a replacement property to be running around like a chicken without its head scratching at the dirt looking for something to buy.

Having said all of this, the lesson to learn is that IRC Section 1031 is still a great loophole. Just ask Donald Trump. He'll tell you that it is, and so will I. All you have to do is get ready well in advance. One of the best ways to do that is to know what you want to buy as a replacement property before you sign the sales agreement on what you are going to give up. If a buyer comes along and you don't want to lose them, make sure you have the right to extend your closing. Many buyers would be happy to get some more "free time," especially if they are going to tear down the existing buildings or need more time themselves to get approvals and the like. Don't rush toward that target day when your 180/45-day clock starts ticking.

But do learn all you can about this great tax loophole.

General Exchanges: Not all real estate exchanges will qualify under IRC Section 1031. That does not mean that a non-1031 exchange is a bad thing to enter into. Sometimes those exchanges can bring a buyer when no buyers seemed to be driving down your street. Let me give you a couple examples of how non-1031 exchanges can work wonders.

Example Number One: Frank owns a tract of land in North Carolina. He isn't really sure now why he purchased it, perhaps it was the fast-talking salesman who convinced Frank that it would be a great spot on which to build a summer home. But for the past 10 years that tract of land has done little but grow pine trees. A local realtor told Frank they'd list it for $150,000, which Frank agreed to, but no buyers came along. Then Frank read one of my books on exchanges, and he realized that he could use that North Carolina property as a catalyst to buy something that would be productive and that might take him closer to one or more of his goals.

Frank listed the tract of land with a Florida broker who was into real estate exchanges. This broker was active in exchange groups, and it was a few weeks after the tract was listed that offers started coming in. They varied a lot. One was the full value of the land for appraised and certified gemstones. Frank said no to that one. Another was a $50,000 value of a sailboat, if Frank would hold an interest only mortgage of $100,000 for 10 years. Frank said no to that one too. Then there came an offer where the other party offered Frank $50,000 of first class airline tickets (that had to be used within three years), and a selection of timeshare units (three worth a total of $40,000) in various places around the world, and the balance of $60,000 was cash.

After some maneuvering with the exchange broker, Frank ended up with the $60,000 in cash, sold $40,000 worth of the airline tickets for $30,000 in cash, and was able to obtain a timeshare in Sedona, Arizona, one in Sapphire Valley, North Carolina, and a third in Orlando, Florida. Each of those locations were favorite places where Frank liked to go, so he was happy and the deal was made.

Example Number Two: Armando has more diamonds than real estate. Of course, Armando has been a good client of mine and has an interesting business. He is a wholesale seller of gemstones. Almost any kind of stone goes through his doors, and I have brokered a number of exchanges with him. The most interesting was a horse farm in Ocala, Florida, which is the horse capital of Florida and is awash with rolling hills and beautiful green pastures. There are large and small horse farms, some just a single-family residence together with a barn and 20 acres of pasture for a horse or two. Others are massive farms of white picket fences with full-sized racing tracks and facilities to train and treat racehorses.

One of the middle-sized farms was offered to my firm. It was too large to be suited as a home with some room for a horse or two, and far too small to appeal to a major operation. The owners asked if we could exchange it for something that could be easily transported to Europe where it could be put into use. In questioning the people who made this inquiry, I discovered that the owner of the horse farm had a fashion design company in Italy. "Could they use certified gem stones?" I asked.

The deal was not easy to put together, after all, gemstones can be hard to evaluate. But in the end the Europeans sent a team of two gemologists who went through a very large selection of various stones and selected $3,250,000 worth of stones at wholesale value and the transaction was completed successfully.

Example Number Three: The Vero Group consisted of 12 individuals of an investment group that purchased a tract of 100 acres with some beach frontage near Vero Beach, Florida. The bottom of the real estate market came the next year, and development seemed to skid to a halt. Interest rates for construction loans were above 20 percent, and all of us in the real estate market were wondering how long it would be before the market sprang back to life.

The group struggled making the payments on the mortgage on the 100 acres, and despite the fact that we had fairly priced the land, no one made an offer. Then one of the broker members in our exchange club asked if we would take 80 acres of land near Naples, Florida as a small part of the deal. The land was part of a very old land development and had paved roads, but no utilities, and some of the land was as close to being a swamp as one might expect.

We ended up discounting the land offered to us down to the rock bottom and took it in the exchange. In the end the deal took us to our goal, which was to sell the Vero land, and within a few years we had moved off the Naples-area land.

There is a simple moral when it comes to real estate exchanges. Make sure you know the value of both what you are giving up and what you get, and any exchange that moves you closer to your goals can be a good exchange. And like most investment techniques, exchanges work for both the buyer and the seller. They are, however, just a technique that should be used when the time is right and the benefits allow one or both of the parties to soften other terms of the deal.

Sweat Equity

Using your own talents to improve real estate or as a down payment can be an excellent start for many new real estate investors. People who are in the building trades have great advantages in this because they have the talent to take a run-down property and to improve it for resale. But sweat equity goes deeper into the creative techniques of the insider real estate investor.

Take Ali, for example. A handyman who frequently did work for me asked me if I knew of any condominiums that he could pick up that needed to be remodeled. It seems he had time on his hands and could do just about anything with building tools.

As I had been paying him on a regular basis for odds and ends work around my office and other property I owned or managed, I suggested that he take a look at a con- dominium that I had recently taken in an exchange as a small part of a bigger deal. It turned out to be very close to where he lived, so he and I struck a deal.

He was to assume a $32,000 mortgage on the property, and as a down payment he would give me $10,000 worth of his handyman labor. The price of $42,000 was fair, and about what I had taken it in exchange for. Other apartments in the complex were selling for more than that, but they had new paint, carpet, and everything worked. Not so with my apartment.

Ali kept the apartment for several years as a rental, and when he decided it was time to move on he had paid down the mortgage to $28,000, was able to put a new mortgage of $46,000 and sold it for $50,000 taking the difference of $4,000 in merchandise from a plumbing store.

An Example of Creative Financing and Its Effect on Cash Flow and/or Equity Buildup

Harry's Option Deal

Remember the discussion of loan to value ratios from Chapter 1. Lenders look to the value of any real estate they take as security for the loan they make. The worth of the property becomes the base value and the loan a percentage of that base. A one million dollar property with a $500,000 loan would be a 50 percent loan to value transaction. A $750,000 loan would be a 75 percent loan to value transaction. The higher the percentage of loan to the total value of the property the greater the risk the lender takes in making the loan. Because of this, whenever the borrower can decrease the loan to value ratio, that borrower increases the change of getting the loan at more favorable rates.

There is another way, however, to achieve the same result without decreasing the actual loan amount. In fact, as you will shortly see, we are going to increase the loan amount while at the same time decreasing the loan to value ratio.

Harry wants to purchase a 30-unit rental apartment complex and to remodel it into an upscale rental, which will cater to young executives that work in the downtown business center two blocks distant. The apartments are on the market for $1,500,000 and will need at least $25,000 per unit in remodeling cost to put the complex in good shape. Harry, who is also a general contractor with his own construction company, knows that he and his two sons can do most of the work themselves, and the total work should not take more than five months to complete. Harry estimates that once the apartment complex is completed, the income will more than double its present level. At that time, the property should support a value of at least $130,000 for each apartment, which would be a total value of $3,900,000. Harry has $750,000, which he can invest in the property, at least $200,000 of that is to pay for the labor (he and his two sons, remember).

He has several choices to follow, and here are two choices he could use to finance this investment.

Choice Number One: He could go to a lender, say a local savings and loan association, and present his cash. No matter what he says, however, here is how the lender will look at this project.

Purchase price	$1,500,000
Cost to remodel at $25,000 each × 30	750,000
Total new value	$2,250,000
Maximum loan to value ratio comfort level	75%
Loan the banker is willing to make	$1,687,500

Now there is nothing wrong with this as a choice. This loan will get Harry all the cash he needs to acquire the property, and he will not spend all his own $750,000 cash to remodel the apartments.

Choice Number Two: On the other hand, if Harry is confident about the ultimate value after his remodeling job, he might choose the following set of events.

Harry negotiates with the seller and enters into an option to purchase the property at $1,350,000. Although this is below the asking price, Harry offers a carrot. He tells the seller that he will spend his own cash to remodel the apartments. He pays the owner $25,000 cash up front, which is applied to the purchase price at the closing. In the agreement, Harry has promised to deposit $725,000 in a local savings and loan, which will pay for the remodeling cost. Remember, some of that cost is going to come right back to Harry because he and his sons own the construction company doing the work and much of the labor will be their own hard work (which they will, of course, get paid for). Harry agrees to a 12-month period, which he knows is a bit more than he should need. If he cannot close on the balance of the purchase price $1,350,000 less the $25,000 option money already paid to the seller, then all the work completed thus far, plus the rest of the money in the account, and the property are kept by the seller.

The owner of the property cannot lose with this situation. He gets to collect rents (until Harry needs the apartments vacant for the remodeling work), and the worst-case scenario might be that Harry fails to complete the work on time, and defaults on the option.

Because the cash paid out comes from Harry's escrowed bank account, earning a small interest rate, he stands the chance of making back the $25,000 option money just from the bank interest. In any event, what Harry is counting on is the final loan from his banker when he has completed the project.

Assume Harry's estimate of the value at the end of 12 months was correct.

Value	$3,900,000
The loan to value comfort level for the lender	75/25
Harry only asks for a 70% loan to value	× 70%
Harry expects a loan of	$2,730,000

Let's review this in light of his new cost in the project.

Option money paid to the seller	$ 25,000
Balance to close on the property	$1,325,000
Total purchase price	$1,350,000

Plus actual materials and labor	750,000
Plus miscellaneous expenses	100,000
Total cash to be invested	$2,200,000
Less recovery of some interest on escrowed funds	25,000
Adjusted cost	$2,175,000
Loan Harry closes on at the bank	$2,730,000
Less Adjusted cost	2,175,000
Harry leaves the closing with this in his pocket	$ 555,000

The point should be clear that Harry did pretty well here. In fact, he did so well that there would have been a lot of room for mistakes for him to still be way ahead of the game.

Now, there is a point of time during this exercise that Harry (or you) would have wanted to make a decision. Was he going to maximize cash flow from this investment or did he want to maximize his equity buildup potential? Let us review what he might have done if he wanted to max out the cash flow from the completed apartments. To set some standards for this review, I have assumed the following: Cash flow return to an investor of 7 percent before income taxes, interest rate on the debt would be 6 percent interest only for 15 years then a balloon would be due (that is really academic here as Harry would have converted this to a condominium prior to that time).

Harry Chooses to Maximize Cash Flow Return

Here is how the proforma for income and expenses would look.

Rents from the 30 apartment units projected at $1,190 per month

Operating expenses at 40% of the gross rents

Harry chooses to borrow only what he actually needs to spend (and he includes what he spends to his own construction company, after all, that is a business and his sons need to get paid, just as does the overhead of the operation). His loan required is $2,175,000. Because the newly remodeled apartments are still at the estimated value of $3,900,000, the loan of $2,175,000 is only slightly over 55 percent of the property value. This would be a highly conservative loan for the lender, and Harry could likely negotiate a very comfortable loan rate. Let's say he gets this loan at 6 percent interest only as I mentioned above. As this is interest, only his payment (based on monthly installments) would be $135,000 for the year.

Presumed value	$3,900,000
Mortgage (100% of Harry's cost)	2,175,000
Value added	$1,725,000

The value added is what has happened to the value of the property, solely because of what Harry did. It does not relate directly back to the cost spent because Harry pulled all of that back out through the financing.

Income and Expenses to Arrive at Cash Flow

Rent from the 30 units at $1,190 per month = annual revenue	$428,400
Less Operating Expenses at 40% of above revenue	170,500
Net operating income	257,900
Debt service (interest only on the $2,175,000 first mortgage)	135,000
Cash flow before income taxes	$122,900

The cash flow of $122,900 is the maximum cash flow under these circumstances. Considering that Harry has zero invested in this project at this point, his return is astronomical. If he chose to, he could retire his existing mortgage in less than 13 years (and that would be without any increase in rents).

If a buyer came along and offered Harry $3,900,000 and paid him $1,725,000 over the existing mortgage, that investor would earn slightly over 7 percent on his cash based on the cash flow of $122,900.

But What If Harry Chooses to Maximize Equity Buildup?

One approach that Harry might make would be to acquire the apartments but not to remodel them into upscale rental apartments. Say that Harry wanted to cash in on the growing condominium market because he knew that anything that was well located would sell at far higher price as a condominium than as its rental counterpart.

Here the numbers may astound you, but the overall risk is not any greater, in my opinion than Harry's more conventional move to cash flow.

Harry and his investment team do their homework and discover that upgraded well-located condominiums in the area can sell for between $280.00 and $300.00 per square foot.

How Does this Relate to This Existing 30-Unit Project?

Thirty two-bedroom, two-bath apartments at 1,260 square feet of area gives the developer a gross saleable area of 37,800 square feet. This multiplied by $280 per square foot produces a potential gross sales of these converted condominiums of $10,584,000.

Harry's Condominium Conversion Approach

Harry estimated that the conversion to condominium would be considerably higher than a simple upgrade to a higher-scale rental that the former building presented. He listed some of the elements that the condominium sales company suggested would be essential.

Lap pool

Large hot-tub Jacuzzi

Fenced deck area around pool and Jacuzzi

All new hardwood doors

New windows

Newly painted inside and out

New electrical outlets and switches

100 percent new kitchens and bathrooms

Hardwood flooring throughout (except bathrooms with ceramic tile)

High-end kitchen and laundry appliances

New central heating and cooling system

Sizable landscape budget

Marketing budget equal to 8 percent of sales

Soft costs equal to 20 percent of all other costs

80 percent acquisition and development loan at 7 percent interest based on sales would mean a loan of $8,467,200 that would be funded when sales reached 60 percent of sales potential.

Interest carry on the loan during construction would be $350,000.

After calculating these costs Harry's cost versus profit numbers looked like this

Harry's Sales Proforma for the Condominium Conversion

Gross sales potential	$10,584,000
Less	
Purchase of the units	$ 1,500,000
Labor and materials	2,900,000
Total hard cost	$ 4,400,000
Marketing	846,720
Debt carry	350,000
Total marketing and debt cost	1,196,720
Total soft cost	1,119,344
Total costs subtracted from sales	$ 6,716,064
Estimated profit from the project (sales less total costs)	$ 3,867,936

Which of these directions would you have chosen?

The more risky of the choices that Harry could take is the condominium conversion, which is also the one that would give him the greatest return. Or would it? First, it is front end loaded. By this I mean that there would be considerable cost that has to be spent before the profit starts to roll in. And when does it start to roll in? Not until the condominiums are completed and there is a certificate of occupancy issued by the local building authorities. This could be two years down the road from the time that Harry started thinking about this project. The risk comes from several directions. They include (but are not limited to) time, delay, cost overruns, and slump in sales of the condominiums, disgruntled lenders, and fear.

It is easy to bump your head on any of those problems. Each has its own special poison, and it is difficult to say which is the worst. It depends on the deal, how deep the investor's pockets really are, and the severity of whichever problem comes up first. I say first because when one problem hits a project there is a very strong likelihood that others are shortly to follow. The last one of my list, "fear," could actually be the first one that occurs, which can end the deal right then and there.

Risk is evident in any real estate transaction. There is no escape from it, there is only the opportunity to see it coming early enough to avoid its consequences. This is why the whole idea of having a comfort zone is critical to the investor's survival. Not only does it build that investor's self-confidence in his or her ability to make the right decisions, it shines through to everyone that person deals with.

CHAPTER 5

Insider Investment Strategies That Increase Cash Flow

The goal of this chapter is:

To Demonstrate Insider Techniques to Increasing Cash Flow

There was a time in my life that was devoted to the study of creative techniques of real estate investing. Those studies evolved into a teaching period of my real estate career with extensive lecture series about that same subject, oriented to the real estate professional. My target audience was realtors and their associates rather than real estate investors. I wanted to give something back to an industry that had, up until then, at least, been very good to me. After all, I rationalized, I really did enjoy helping people fulfill their economic dreams through real estate investing, and helping other brokers and salesmen and women do the same was my way of a positive payback. It was timely too, because the real estate market was in one of its down cycles and being creative really did help buyers acquire property and helped sellers move on to other things. Then real estate suddenly got so hot that real estate salespeople began to become more like order takers than salespersons or even qualified advisors. Sadly, this tends to be a negative side effect of a booming economy, and for the past seven years, (for me anyway) real estate has been the golden goose that lays the golden egg of financial independence.

However, real estate cycles change, and we are about to enter a transition from a truly hot market in most places of the country, to a far milder market. Keep in mind that I have cautioned about up and down cycles not occurring at the same time for different categories of real estate, especially when viewed over the wide spectrum of a large diverse area. By area I mean any large area where different elements that effect the value of real estate can occur in such a way that values of one category of real estate may go up on one side of town and down on the other side. Most certainly, this would happen in different cities within a state. Be careful to look beyond published statistics when making comparisons of markets in different areas. Higher or lower percentages of home construction by region of the United States, for example, may reflect weather conditions and not an economic decline of the market.

It is very important that any investor who expands her sights beyond what she knows, such as her comfort zone, continue to be mindful of that Green Grass Syndrome I have mentioned in an earlier chapter. But what looks like a green pasture does appear all the time and that event, plus the inability to apply creative techniques that work (for both buyer and seller) are essential to the real estate investor who wants to survive the down cycles of the market.

All real estate investors, whether they are buyers or sellers, also need to remember that markets vary from place to place. This is the essence of the Green Grass Syndrome. A good example of how this works happened to me today. A good client of mine, for whom I have assembled properties and helped with development, has become an expert in the conversion of rental apartments into residential condominiums for sale. His comfort zone is the Fort Lauderdale area, expanding into some of the small towns that border Fort Lauderdale, but not farther away than that.

He knows this market very well, understands the politics there, and what it should cost to buy, develop and market. Best of all, he knows what price point works best (the price of the product), for the buyers present.

Whatever he buys and develops in Fort Lauderdale at this time, he needs to sell at a minimum of $350 per square foot. He has based this on the fact that every 1,400-square foot apartment (non high-rise of less than eight floors high) will cost him between $185 to $210 per square foot to build (total of hard cost, soft cost that includes marketing, sales commissions and financing) plus between $70,000 to $125,000 per unit for the land and approvals to develop (this includes basic land cost, architects, engineers, lawyers, traffic studies, and so on).

Therefore, actual acquisition and total development and sales for each 1,400-square foot apartment will look like this:

Summary of Development Costs and Marketing and Resulting Profit

Item	Low Prices	High Prices
Land cost	$ 70,000	$125,000
Total development cost	259,000	294,000
Land and development cost	$329,000	$419,000
Sales at $350 per sq. foot	$490,000	$490,000
Less land and development cost	329,000	419,000
Projected profit per unit	$161,000	$ 71,000
Profit as a % of sales price	33%	14%

When you look at these numbers, you might assume that this kind of real estate investing is a can't lose kind of investing, if every project works exactly within those parameters. Why even a 14 percent return from gross sales can be a good margin. In good times with people who know what they are doing that is right. Nevertheless, that last sentence is filled with potential disasters. Things go wrong, and it is not difficult to make several mistakes in a row (because one mistake tends to cause another) that add up to additional cost, and a less than expected sales volume. Therefore, if property costs more to buy and develop than anticipated and sells for less than you need to get, it is not all that difficult to lose money, or to be forced to cut your potential loss and close down the sales office before construction starts.

Mistakes generally occur in real estate investing, when timing is in the way. Try to get something done to a tight deadline, and mistakes follow; count on something that should take 6 months and it will take 14. That can happen when things are not absolutely 100 percent going for you.

Okay, back to what happened to me today. While this condominium conversion expert was in my office, we were reviewing a rental apartment complex for sale in the Tampa, Florida, area. It is a 120-unit complex in a modest working class and student housing community serving the massive University of South Florida, half a dozen hospitals, several major shopping malls, as well as the famous Busch Gardens amusement park. It is fed by good traffic streets, a major interstate highway two blocks away, and downtown Tampa 15 minutes to the south.

Based on the idea of a 1,400-square-foot apartment, the product (already developed but 26 years old) would cost $78,000 and is in grave need of a substantial upgrade. The price point for the neighborhood as a newly fixed up (but not fully rehabilitated with new designer kitchens and bathrooms), would be $130,000 to $160,000 and not a penny more. Already you should see the benefit of knowing what will sell in which part of the world. This price point clearly ruled out Fort Lauderdale development mentality. Even at $160,000 per apartment (of 1,400 square feet), we are talking about only $114.00 per square foot, and not the $350 per square foot that Fort Lauderdale developers have moved to (at this time).

Although the economics of Tampa might be close to that of Fort Lauderdale as for new well-located condominiums, (say downtown or on the beach, river, or estuary), the conversion of existing rental apartments is a different story. Why? Because virtually every older rental complex of 50 or more apartments in Fort Lauderdale area has already been converted, whereas in Tampa conversion is just starting in earnest.

Review the Tampa Conversion Project

Selling price	$160,000
Purchase price of the unit predevelopment:	$ 78,000
Rehab	33,410
Total cost to acquire and rehab	111,410
Breakdown of rehab cost	
Central air and heat	$ 2,600
Midrange kitchen, redo	6,000
New appliances	3,500
Electrical upgrade	400
New carpet	2,800
New front door	500
Tile in bathroom and kitchen	950
Paint inside and out	1,900
Landscaping budget	1,500
Overall complex redo	4,500
Overhead	2,500
Marketing cost, 8% of sales	1,760
Miscellaneous	2,500
Cost of debt	2,000
Projected Profit	$ 48,590
Profit as a % of sales	30+%

Here we are, looking at two different markets in the same state at the very same time. One has a very high price point ($350 per square foot) the other is much lower, $114.00 per square foot. In addition, because the acquisition of the product plus development cost is so much different, the profit in the Tampa product is much greater than that of Fort Lauderdale. However, which is the better investment?

The answer to that question is very simple. Which opportunity comes to you first, and which do you really want to undertake, if you would be qualified to do either one. Many investors will not go ten miles from where they live. That person would make decisions based on geographic boundary. The investor who will never touch a remodel job (because there are hidden problems there) will simply walk away from that kind of situation. The Tampa developer who has made money (say last year) with a similar project as outlined above in the Tampa area, would be frightened to death of trying a similar venture in Fort Lauderdale because the comfort level would be with the lower price point. Equally, it should be evident that while the discussion is of development of condominium apartments, the conversion of an older rental is not the same thing as a new development project. The most significant difference between the two kinds of developments is location, use, and approval.

A developer may compromise in selecting a conversion of an older property because the location will generally be suitable for a known price point, the use would likely fit the zoning, which means that approvals can be far quicker and easier than battling it out with the local planning and zoning board. On the other hand, when the price point for the product that the investor is comfortable with does not work, the task shifts to a search for a location where it will work. This opens the door for more potential mistakes because of the time it takes to carry such a project forward. By the time the site is found, put under contract, and approvals are obtained, the sales market (perhaps two years later)—the market for the price point needed to meet the total cost and still provide a profit—may have dried up.

So here we are, opening the doors for you so that you look deeper than the surface and so that you look for the answers before you need to know them. What kind of answers? Where have you been? You need to know the zoning, the building codes and regulations, and you must establish a working relationship with the officials in the local government that control these important elements: zoning, building, permits, fire codes, density (as for multifamily uses) and influence in the community. Okay, I have not mentioned this last element before. Who is that person? Well it is really a mix of people, the mayor, the local commissioners, especially the one that is in charge of the area where the property in question is located, the state senator of that district, the federal senator and representative to congress from that area, the head of the immediate police and fire departments, and the governing tax assessor.

Get to know those important people on a first-name basis. I know, it is not an overnight process, but it is far easier than you might think. They are all local politically motivated people. Most are either actually voted in, or nominated or hired by those people who are voted in. They listen to and lean toward the people who may, some day, vote them (or their sponsors) out of office.

Terms and Concepts You Need to Know

The Four Postures of Property Management

In my book *Commercial Real Estate Investing* published by John Wiley & Sons in 2004, I discuss the four postures of property management. Any one of these postures has its place as the right choice to follow, based on the goals the property owner is striving to reach. Applying the wrong kind of management can greatly increase operational expenses, and that will take a big bite out of the potential cash flow of the property. The best approach is to anticipate what the result needs to be. With that clearly in mind, both interim and long-range goals can be made and focus can be directed to the management that best reaches the goal, while producing the highest cash flow possible in the meanwhile. Look at these four methods of management.

Management Posture 1: Do nothing to maintain the property. There are few real estate investments that benefit from this management posture. Some exceptions however would be vacant land, or buildings that are very soon to be torn down to make way for a new project. You might suggest that property that is leased to a tenant who must maintain the property to strict standards would also fit, but it is the actual management of the property that I am talking about, so that situation would actually fit as management posture 3.

Vacant land can become management intensive if it is to be ultimately used in a development of some kind, or if the investor is working through a rezoning process with the local authorities or is in the actual planning of a development and following through with it. Long-term ownership of vacant land that is "land banked" for a use that is five years or more in the future also needs to have a management program geared more to an upgrade mode where the land is either put into temporary agriculture production or planted with potential future landscape material. Both of those temporary uses can provide tax savings when the local taxing authority has tax exemptions for land in agricultural uses, as well as create some cash flow from the sale of crops, timber, or benefit from the maturing of landscape material that will actually be used in the final development.

However, the idea of doing nothing to a property while it increases in value by itself is an attractive alternative to management intensive investments. For this reason, speculation in raw land is attractive, and when investments are prudently made, they can be very profitable.

There is a risk, however, in making real estate investments where the investor anticipates that the property will not be put to its ultimate use for several years or longer. The risk is that when the appointed time arrives there will be difficulties that need to be overcome that did not exist when the property was acquired. These difficulties may involve zoning changes, moratoriums on development, or lack of utilities or other services that render development impossible, or costly.

Management Posture 2: Do very little to maintain the property unless something is actually broken; then fix it only if necessary. In the end, this form of management will run a property into the ground, but is the right choice of management for a property that is in a temporary use mode. For example, if you purchased a motel with the idea of converting it to a nursing home, or some other use in a couple of years, this management posture will enable it to continue to function as a motel until the conversion to the new use commences. Because you know in advance what you need to change during the conversion process, management of property and personnel can be selective and minimal. The correct approach in this kind of situation is to have a plan that gets the most out of the property without having to be replaced. The last thing you would want to do is to have to replace major elements of a property, such as an elevator system, or central airconditioning equipment a year before you are going to gut the building and convert it to another use. Unless, those replacements would actually fit the needs of the new use.

Management Posture 3: Maintain the property in its original good condition. This is the management posture that you, as an investor, would want your triple net tenants to be responsible for. In a long-term real estate investment you anticipate that the underlying land will be the basis for appreciation of the asset. The idea that a day will come when the buildings will be worthless and the land far more valuable than the existing use of the facilities is a real one and can easily be the long-range result. There are many uses that produce good cash flow and require only minimal investment in facilities. These can include parking lots, car lots (both new and used), vehicle and boat storage lots, landscape sales facilities and so on. All can be temporary cash flow producers for many years as the land continues to outstrip the value of buildings.

When a city enters a renewal stage, the downtown area becomes the battleground for developers. They battle to acquire old structures, raze them, and build a new city. At times like this, it is not uncommon for property (land and buildings) that could be purchased a year or two earlier for several hundred thousand dollars to suddenly have a new economic potential and a new value, worth many millions of dollars.

I brokered a transaction four years ago with a local property owner for a five-acre tract of land, a whole city block actually, near the downtown area of Fort Lauderdale. The agreed to price was just under $8 million.

The investor went through the right motions, but did not really have his heart in the deal after the city planning office said there was not a chance in a million that he would get an approval for the 380 apartment units and 40,000 square feet of commercial space that he wanted to build. Therefore, the deal fell apart.

Exactly 24 months later, this same investor reconsidered, and came back to the table and the buyer and seller agreed on a price of ten million dollars. Then one of those unfortunate snags developed. Before the seller's trustee could get back in town (from his Caribbean cruise) to sign the contract of sale, another developer in town jumped into the transaction and offered 18 million dollars. The seller, jumped for the much larger deal and took it. Another two years passed, bringing us back to this moment. The new developer fought things out with the city and got more than 430 condominium units approved, with nearly the 40,000 square feet of commercial space. This new developer could easily sell the whole package to any number of other developers in the country who would jump for the chance to have a "cooked deal" that has full approvals, building plans in hand, and is ready to go. How much would someone pay for that package? At least $34,000,000 and perhaps more.

What happened was the original owner who had the property for nearly 20 years had managed it in management posture 1 and 2. The buildings eventually were in such poor condition that they had been removed, and the land was a vacant eyesore. Then new investors appeared with different management postures in mind because they saw a situation where new value could be added to the equation just by getting approvals for a new project or use.

The ultimate profit will come from the actual implementation of those approvals through the next management posture.

Management Posture 4: Maintain the property in a constant upgrade mode. As in the example just given, it is important to remember that upgrade mode does not just mean improving the buildings or aesthetics of the property. An economic improvement of the potential of the property can bring the highest return on the actual investment.

Most investors will have to balance their management postures to improve the property while still generating cash flow. Improvements must be viewed from the return they can produce, while not becoming a lost asset when they are removed from the property to make way for a new use too early in their life.

Most of us have seen relatively new buildings torn down to make way for a different use. There are some uses that are so cash flow intensive that they overshadow the value of existing facilities that are, in their own right, profitable. One example of such a use is the modern drug store. These are not really drug stores at all. They are really a small pharmacy surrounded by massive retail departments that have a little of just about everything you might need, plus a million items of things that you never think of buying until you get there. They seem to spring up everywhere as long as one of the competition is directly across the street. Large office buildings of a hundred thousand feet of office space are torn down to make way for a 50,000 square foot chain drug store.

Steady improvement and up grading of a property takes careful planning to be cost effective and to maintain the continuity of the original investment goals. If an investment is made with the idea of building a well run profitable resort hotel, then there should be a master plan early on that enables the upgrades to occur in the order that will get the most out of them. Poor management in upgrading a property can mean that elements introduced may later conflict with other upgrades, and the whole process can be like a Latin dance where for every three steps forward there must be two steps to the rear.

The key is to have a goal and to manage toward that goal. Success comes from having a vision of the final product and proceeding toward the vision.

Properties with the Best Potential
to Increase the Cash Flow

As you develop your comfort zone, you will begin to see things in that geographic area that have always been there, although you didn't know what you were actually looking at. The following should become your checklist of the best choice of properties that may offer potential for increased cash flow. Often only one of the factors in this list will stand out (sometimes like a sore thumb), but when you dig a bit more into the circumstances of the property you will find a combination of events taking place. It will be important for you to question why to each such event. Once you believe you know why things are what they are, you then need to ask yourself: "Can I fix this and generate revenue and profits that do not currently exist?" If you cannot, or do not want to take on that task, for whatever reason, drop the would-be project and move on. There will always be another deal out there somewhere.

Properties with Potential for Increased Cash Flow

Poorly managed properties.

Current rents are below market rates.

Simple and cheap improvements warrant rent increases.

New and positive infrastructure is on the way.

Properties with economic conversion potential.

Poorly Managed Properties

Instead of seeing the rental apartment complex that looks a bit tired and run down, you see what the real problem is at that location. The management has allowed a bad mix of tenants to take over the property. Trash appears overnight, old cars with flat tires are scattered around the parking areas, and vacancy rates are high and rental income low. What you really see is the opportunity for good management to take this property and turn it around.

Current Rents Are below Market Rates

Often the turnaround is not very difficult. If you know the rental market for your area, you may easily recognize that there is substantial potential to just move the current rent roll up from the average of $650 per month to $850 per month. The effort to do this may not take a long time, and it may be relatively inexpensive. The key is to have a plan that takes the property through the essential stages that will give the desired results. It would be a mistake, for example, to jump into a property like this and to start making major improvements to the facility itself without first addressing the cause of the problem, which likely is a combination of bad management and bad tenant mix. When neither the management nor the tenants have any pride in their living conditions, to improve the conditions without getting rid of the old tenants is a waste of time, money, and investment capital.

Simple and Cheap Improvements Warrant Rent Increases

The development plan to turn an old, tired-looking property around should start with the most basic of all elements. This would be a full and complete audit of all leases, so that you would have an accurate picture of the make up of tenants and their history of payments, problems, and lease termination dates. Any tenant that falls into the problem tenant category should be given a lease termination notice as soon as possible. At the same time, a general clean up of the visual deterioration of the facilities should begin. The combination of these two events sends a powerful signal to all the tenants, as well as potential new tenants. This property is going to see a change for the better.

These initial improvements need not be very costly, providing that your prepurchase due diligence has not turned up any major problems. It is okay to have major problems, though, as long as you recognize what they are, when they need to be attended to, how much it will cost to fix them, and that you have adjusted your acquisition price accordingly. It is the surprises that can hurt you, such as finding out that your inspection team forgot to check the plumbing or central heating system, or some other costly item to be repaired or replaced.

While the general clean up is underway, the overall plan should be devised and divided into stages that allow the flow of work to progress so that things do not occur that get undone by work that follows. Landscape gets finished at the end of the project, but some elements can start early. This would be especially so if any large trees are to be introduced. It is easier and far less expensive to be able to move such elements around a project before new walkways, a swimming pool, tennis court, or children's playground, or even sod or hedges are put into place.

The key here is to:

1. Know the rental market for the area around this property

2. Know what must be done to get the maximum rent from the area

3. Have a budget for the work that fits those needs

4. Have a realistic proforma that takes into account the cost of the time it will take to meet the increased revenue expectations

5. Have the combination of capital (both yours and OPM) to meet the cost

6. Hire professionals to do the planning

New and Positive Infrastructure Is on the Way

When something new is about to happen to an area, property values are bound to be impacted. This means they can and will go either up or down or both for any specific location. By location, I mean that very specific locations near the new infrastructure may rise in value, while others go down. Equally, sometimes the values first go one way, then reverse and go the other.

Good examples of this occur when new traffic ways are introduced or improved. One of the worst things that can happen to a nice commercial street, lined on both sides with upscale shops and hotels, is for the road to be widened with new storm sewers installed, and major landscaping relocated. Projects like this may have a bright future for the area, but only at the end of three years of a construction mess. During the mess time, businesses close, property owners, with little or no income have to sell, and opportunities arise for the investor who knows what will occur at the end of this horrible time in the life of that property.

While the more adversely affected properties drop in value (although only temporarily), a block or two away other properties may start to rise in value in anticipation of their new value as sites for new projects that will be unaffected by the construction mess.

Because there is often a very long delay between the time any new infrastructure project is planned to when it even starts, the investor who is watching for these events can have a head start on taking advantage of what is sure to happen. Sure to happen, that is, if the timing is right. Most people, even property owners in the area about to be affected, do not react, or at least fully react, until the construction team actually arrives and the DETOUR sign goes up.

Most infrastructure will have different effects on different categories of real estate usage. A mammoth new University (this happens) that is planned for a 300-acre site of land will have very interesting benefits, both for the long term and nearly instantly. Any new employment center will have similar impacts and can present the savvy investor with a choice of opportunities.

When the employment center or other development is nongovernmental, such as a new Cyber Software Industrial Park, the investor needs to exercise caution, especially when the developer is looking for community concessions to build the project. The reason for this is there are many communities that actively seek such development, and there is often considerable competition between the communities (even states) to attract such development. The developer or sponsor for this development will play each community against the other and sometimes make a sudden move from Georgia to Florida (or the other way around) to take advantage of a better economic result.

Properties with Economic Conversion Potential

Because of any of the above events may be happening, one of the best properties to take advantage of would be anything that had economic conversion potential. For example, if the main street has been shut down for 6 months already, with another 12 to follow, you might find a nice office building that has been losing tenants steadily for those 6 months. By now the property owner will see the possibility that trend will continue at least until the construction has been completed. If this building had potential to be converted to a condominium office building, or an office building that catered to one specific category of business, like a medical building or legal center, then this might be a good direction to go. Of course, a combination of those two, a condo medical complex, as an example, could be even better.

As construction costs continue to rise at an astronomical pace, an older well-constructed building may present a cheaper way to go than to start from scratch. It is interesting that some buildings that were built before 1940 may have special features that present real perks to the conversion investor. Higher ceilings may exist, as well as larger spaces without supporting walls in the interior of the building. The absence of supporting walls makes it easy to gut the interior of a building and reconfigure partitioning walls to suit the new use. Naturally, the ability to comply inexpensively with current building codes will be critical to the overall cost of a new project. Generally, the most expensive to meet will be fire codes. To this end, the older buildings may actually lend themselves to less expensive means to do this if their ceilings are high and there is an absence of interior supporting walls. The costs to bring elevator and fire escape stairwells up to code are also major elements that any remodeling or conversion plan must ascertain.

The most important thing to remember in a conversion of any kind is to avoid being the pioneer of such events in any area. It is far better to follow in the footsteps of the first few such pioneers. In real estate, many millionaires have been made by riding on the coattails of the first successful guy.

Nine Comfort Zone Bonanzas That Point Toward Increased Cash Flow

It will be helpful if you keep this list of comfort zone bonanzas in mind as you make your frequent rounds of your chosen comfort zone.

Additional Density Available

Estate and Court Ordered Sales

For Sale by Owner

Hidden Gems

Hot Neighborhood

Lender's REO

Out of Town Owners

Overgrown Yard

Victim of a Calamity

Review each of these items in detail.

Additional Density Available

By the time you have selected the geographic area of your comfort zone, you will be on your way to discover just how important is your knowledge of the zoning ordinances and building rules and regulations. It is a good idea to have a zoning map with you whenever you are making your rounds of this investment area. The principal reason for this is that you may not be able to pinpoint the exact point where one zone changes, or even remember which street you were on, if you wait until you get back to your office or home to doublecheck things. One of these truly important things you will discover is that some properties you locate are not developed to their full potential. For example, you are driving through your area and pass a 15-unit apartment complex you have seen a million times. Only now, you check the zoning map, and realize that the property is zoned for 40 units to the acre. You doublecheck your Platt of the same area and realize that the property is approximately two acres in size. That means that if the existing buildings were torn down or added to in some way, there could be a potential total of 80 units on the site. I caution you to use the word "potential" because even though the zoning says it's okay, there might be some other restriction that would block that full use. It could be a building code that says that due to a natural gas line that runs through the property no building can be constructed within 100 feet of the line. Unless you could make arrangements to move the line (and this could be possible, although expensive, but worth finding out), the existing 15 units might be it. Or perhaps not it after all.

Other forms of density include commercial density that sometimes, just like multifamily density, is tied to a Floor Area Ratio formula (called simply FAR). Depending on how the building authorities calculate—and it can vary between cities in the same county—this is a formula based on the total area of the property times a multiple that is established for a specific area or zoning. For example, say the zoning was 4FAR; this would mean that the approved density of square feet of building would be four times the area of the land. The area of the land can be calculated in several different ways too, so it is important to know which method that building authority uses. Here are several ways this can be calculated, and while one of these is likely, your building department may have invented something new in the way they calculate things, so check first. Once the area of the site (which is allowed for the purposes of FAR or Density) has been ascertained, then the developer would apply the rules as to what is excluded from that allowable square footage to know what he can build. When FAR applies to multifamily uses (apartments, hotels, town homes, and so forth) the square footage allowed would be spread over the total area, and a per unit count would not (usually) be used.

Area by Survey: The accurate survey of the real estate is what you own and will reflect a square footage. If the property is 200 feet × 600 feet in size, you will have a surveyed square footage of 120,000 square feet. As one acre is 43,560 square feet, this site consists of 2.7548 acres (120,000 divided by 43,560 = 2.7548). If the building department used this as your site square footage, then a 4FAR (or FAR4), would total 4 × 120,000 = 480,000 square feet of building. This might relate to 480 1,000-square-foot apartments or a combination of a certain amount of offices and the balance in some residential use. Just to show you the difference between FAR and per acre density, if this were multifamily zoning at a density of 40 units per acre, you would be able to build 40 × 2.7548 acres = 110 units.

By Lot Line to Center of Road Measurements: This is a different method to arrive at square footage of a site. Say the above 200 foot × 600 foot property was a corner on two major streets and each had a right-of-way of 200 feet (distance to cross the street to the other side and would include swale and sidewalks and any other unpaved area and not just the asphalted road). Some building authorities allow the site size for the purposes of both density and FAR to extend to the center of any road that fronts any border of the site. In the case of the site in question, we would now have measurements of the survey itself, as well as the area from the property line to the centerline of the street. This would give us a measurement of 200 + 100 feet = 300 feet for one measurement, and 600 + 100 feet = 700 feet for the other. 300 × 700 = 210,000 feet for the site. This is much larger than the actual surveyed area. With a 4FAR (4 × 210,000) we now have 840,000 square feet of potential building allowable. The 210,000 square feet of size of the site (for these purposes) would amount to 4.8209 acres, which at 40 units per acre would allow 192 units.

By Buildable Square Footage: This is the maximum footprint which would be allowed if the FAR or Density was restricted by setback requirements. So far, this is the most restrictive of all methods described. To ascertain this, you must know setbacks of any building from the survey boundaries. These setbacks may vary on the same site, depending on what is being built, so you would have to find in the building code all the kinds of uses that would go on the property according to the zoning, then double check each use to required setbacks. For example, a business zoning might allow several dozen different uses, and spread across them might be several setback requirements. Often, there are just one setback criteria, however, which simplifies things. In this case, and as an example, let's say our 200×600 foot property has setbacks of 50 feet from any road (we have a corner remember), and 20 feet from other sides that border other property and not a road. Our buildable site is now, $200'$ less $50' + 20' = 130'$ for one dimension and the other $600'$ less $50' + 20' = 530'$. The total area buildable area is now $130' \times 530'$ or a footprint of 68,900 square feet. Therefore, the 4FAR would allow 4 times 68,900 square feet or a total of 275,600 square feet of building. If this was also the density calculation at 40 units per acre, we would have 1.581 acres $\times$ 40 or only 63 total units allowable.

By Site Plan Approval: Most communities have a process where a developer can present the project for approval by site plan. Sometimes the planning and zoning department may insist on projects of a certain magnitude going through this process. It has a lot of advantages to the developer if the local politics and attitude toward development are on the favorable side, and vice versa. Here both parties either work together to get the most out of the development (not always the biggest, but what is best for the area, the tax base of the community with compromises being made by each side along the way). The rules of zoning, and building even setbacks can be ignored or most certainly modified to meet these ends. Here it is pure and simple a dog and pony show between the developer and those who must vote on the project. The developer usually is asked (or forced) to meet with the local home owners in the surrounding area of the project, and if the end result is continued or increased opposition from those homeowners, the project may not pass the muster of approval without a change or many changes by the developer.

Some developers get to that point, after many thousands of dollars of expense, only to be unable to justify the changes they must make to get approval, and they walk away from the project.

Now, having gone through these different methods, there are several elements that can apply to the first three in the FAR calculations (and rarely multifamily density). These are public area, structured parking, green area, and dry area retention.

Public Area: This is the area of a building that consists of halls, lobby area, bathrooms, elevator and stair shafts and other space (if any) that is excluded from what would be considered as tenant or owner-occupied space. Some FAR calculations exclude all public area from the FAR calculation. This means that if we calculate 480,000 square feet of building allowed, then we would not have to include the public area within that square footage.

Structured Parking: This includes any parking garage that is constructed anywhere on the site. Like the public area, structured parking may not need to be included in the allowable FAR buildable space. In the case of 480,000 square feet of allowable space, the parking required for that space may be exempt and not included in that space.

Green Area: This is an area that by building code must be left in landscaping and "open" to the sky. Some codes require this to be at grade level (close to street level) of the property, whereas some codes allow it to be elevated, say on the top of a garage or a combination of the two.

Dry Area Retention: This is a new term for most parts of the country and deals with the ability of a site to retain water from rain. This is important in areas where there is no storm drainage (or none allowed for certain sites), in order to keep a large fully paved shopping center from sending thousands of gallons of its rainwater to flood the homes behind it. There are some ways to mitigate these areas, such as special drains to pipes that are buried under parking lots to allow the water to soak into the land under that asphalt. However, that can be very expensive, and the land itself may not "perk" (allow the water to soak at a fast enough rate to qualify). When the local building authorities require a developer to provide dry area retention, the actual area it takes to meet the water storage requirement may eat up so much of the real estate that the size of the building (square feet or density count) may not be possible. This can be an economic blow to the value of the property, and an investor who has done all his homework (except the dry area retention requirement) may have purchased land that will not fit his needs, even though the zoning has given the green light to move forward.

The end result for this long explanation is to demonstrate why this very important factor about real estate is often overlooked by investors—either overlooked or simply miscalculated. A miscalculation here could make a great difference between the size of rentable or saleable space or the number of apartments allowed.

The first couple of times you go through this exercise, I would recommend you be at the building department's desk, talking to one of the officials there. Have a site in question, and let them walk you through the process. Most such officials will take the time to do this, especially if you are nice to them. They are used to people who are not so nice and respond accordingly.

Because as sure as horses like to eat apples, you will begin to find situations in your comfort zone that are clearly zoned for something else or for more than what you see. This is the beginning for you to start to see the budding trees in the forest long before they have broken ground.

Estate or Court Ordered Sales

An estate or court ordered sale is the result of a death or other action that results in a less than voluntary sale. Generally there is strong motivation on the part of the parties to resolve the situation. You will want to keep your eyes open for such opportunities. As you learn more about your comfort zone, you will also start to learn who owns what property there. The properties you are most interested in will be those you research early in your development of the zone. You may even know or meet some of these owners, so you would likely notice when one dies or is a party to a legal action that results in a court-ordered sale. It is a good idea to check your newspaper from time to time in the legal notices sections. Deaths, partnership breakups, divorce settlements, foreclosures, and the like are all potential sources of motivated sellers. A motivated seller is often a source of a good deal.

For Sale by Owner

Owners who put a sign up that says they want to sell are crying for help. They either have given up on the real estate profession, or want to try to save a commission by selling the property themselves. Dealing with sellers can be frustrating because they may not have negotiation skills and can become "insulted" as a result. As a broker, I wish I had a thousand dollars for every seller who told me he was insulted at an offer I was presenting on behalf of a buyer I represented. "Mr. Seller," I would begin, "this person thinks enough of your property to want to own it. In fact, the two of you should be glad you are meeting. After all, you have what he wants to buy, and as a buyer he can solve your need to sell." Usually I would pause then continue. "If you are insulted by his offer, then let's work together to see if I can bring the two of you together. Don't be angry at him, rather, direct your anger at those people who have not been interested enough to even make an offer."

Nonetheless, the motivated seller has the potential to help you buy the property. I recommend that when you deal with such people either be sure to have very good negotiation skills (and charm to boot) or have a good broker who can be the buffer between the two principals.

Hidden Gems

Not every property has hidden gems, but many have more than one of those on this list. By the way, this is not the exclusive list of such elements, which exist in buildings or on property. Some areas of the country may have coal deposits a few feet under the ground, others may even sit right in the middle of a gold field. Who knows what lurks in the shadows of your real estate. Here is a partial list of such hidden gems. You will not necessarily know they exist without a complete inspection of the property. Oh, if you do notice one or more of these items, do not gush about and let the whole world (or the seller for that matter) know that the things you find are important to you. They may have taken them so much for granted that they have no real value to them at all.

Well

Attic that is usable/finished

Boat dock

City natural gas to the property

Crawl space under the floor

Dry and finished basement

Famous neighbors (past, present, or future)

Great views (from the roof)

Hurricane or storm shutters

Impact glass

Moveable built-ins

No internal support walls

Real brick under paint

Stone, wood, or ceramic tile floors under carpet

Storm shelter

Swimming pool

Valuable landscape you hate

Wood floors

Hot Neighborhood

A hot neighborhood is one that is going through a transition for the better. Investors have noticed this and are rushing in to ride those coattails I mentioned earlier. There will come a time when it might be too late to be the developer who makes money here. When that happens, things will taper off for a while and then start up again until all the old properties have been recycled. As events move toward that tapering off time, it will be more critical to stay on top of both construction costs and both the rental market (for the area) and what price point the buyers will accept.

If your comfort zone does not include a hot neighborhood, look around for one. This will serve two important purposes. First, it will give you input as to what happens, when it happens, and when it stops happening in a hot neighborhood. This knowledge will pay off elsewhere, even if it does not actually work for you in this new part of your comfort zone. Secondly the more you know about what is going on in your real estate market, the better you are to avoid Green Grass Syndrome.

Lender's REO

All lenders either have a real estate owned department (REO) or farm their property out to real estate firms to handle sales of these properties. These are properties a lender has taken back, either by voluntary deed in lieu of foreclosure, or actual foreclosure itself.

Lenders are motivated sellers, and they are lenders too. This combination makes for excellent negotiation and can result with some very attractive transactions. Many lenders are also joint venture players, or can be enticed to work with you at a very fair price and terms if they can get a piece of the action (after you have already made your profit, too).

Best of all, lender REO officers are accessible. In fact, if they are not, they do not keep their jobs very long.

Out of Town Owners

Property that is owned by people who live at a distance from the real estate may not stay on top of what is going on in the neighborhood. This simple fact may give you an edge in taking advantage of some new or fast breaking news that will have a positive impact to the value or use of property in your comfort zone. Check the tax assessor's web page for your area. If the tax assessor's office has not developed online access to its information, a personal visit to their office will ultimately give you all the information you need to ascertain where the owner of any real estate in your comfort zone lives. The tax assessor's office has this information because they send the tax bill to the owner every year. It is a good idea to become familiar with the services and data that are available to any member of the public from the tax assessor's office. You will discover tax assessed value, the property tax, recent sales information, square footage of the property, and (generally) buildings. There may also be maps and plat information that shows you zoning.

Overgrown Yard

Even with a quick drive through your comfort zone, you may discover evidence of neglect. This usually shows up first by the condition of the yard, which has not been maintained for several months. This can be the sign that something has happened to the owners of the property, or that a tenant has left the property. Whenever this becomes evident, you want to attempt to contact the owner. Even if you were not interested in buying this property, at this time, you might make a great contact by asking the owners if there is anything you could do to help them. This would be especially neighborly if the owner of the property lived out of town.

Victim of a Calamity

Property severely damaged by a storm or other event may produce a windfall for both the owner and you, if you were looking for property in the area. This would certainly be the case if your interest was to tear down a building in order to construct a new property at that location. In Florida, old hotels or other buildings that are sitting on oceanfront land, for example, are regularly torn down to make way for oceanfront condominiums. The owners of these properties that are gravely damaged by a storm may take advantage of their insurance proceeds to sell the property at that time, rather than rebuild or repair the damaged property. The insurance company will attempt to negotiate a reduction in their insurance awards, but the combination of insurance (whatever the owner gets) and a buyer glad to get the property, may result in a good deal for everyone.

Dealing with insurance companies on such settlements is time consuming and is best handled by a lawyer or other person that has knowledge and experience of these kinds of transactions.

Alexander's Example of a Mixed Technique Purchase to Maximize and Increase Cash Flow

Alexander is an experienced real estate investor who has been around Miami for a long time. He has a large portfolio of rental properties that include apartments (both buildings and individual condos he rents out), single-family homes, and commercial buildings. He has enough property to keep two handymen in full-time employment doing repairs, upgrades, and new additions to existing properties. The following is an example of how he used several different techniques in a recent acquisition. His comfort zone ranges over much of Miami-Dade County, Florida, which is where Miami is located. Although he has owned property throughout Dade County, he specializes in the older sections of south Miami, Coconut Grove, and Coral Gables.

He had been admiring a 21-unit apartment building that is located in the town of Coral Gables, which adjoins Miami. From the tax assessor's office and the city building and zoning office, Alexander had discovered that the building was constructed in 1951, and its three floors of apartments consisted of 18 two-bedroom two-bath apartments and three three-bedroom three-bath apartments. The property was only three short blocks from the main shopping area of Coral Gables, and the site had been rezoned by the city in the late 1950s to accommodate future high-rise mixed use of residential condominiums as well as office and other commercial uses. The existing owners purchased the property in 1978 for $945,000, and in 1993 installed fire sprinklers throughout the building, and had remodeled the building to accommodate an elevator system plus central air conditioning for each apartment. The cost of these improvements was $225,000.

The square footage of the building including halls, storage, stairs and elevator shafts was just over 36,000 square feet. Alexander will ultimately use the following techniques in his acquisition of this property:

Sweat Equity Lease

Option to Buy

Sliding Mortgage

Interest Only Debt

Economic Conversion

Let us follow what he did.

Sweat Equity Lease

An opportunity to meet the owners of the property had come several years earlier when they actually contacted Alexander about property management. They had enquired if he managed properties other than the ones he owned, having gotten his name from a sign on one of his buildings that read "Newly Remodeled Apartments for Rent." This sign, by the way, was one of many such signs that Alexander had installed on all of his properties. Even when a building was fully occupied, the sign would pull prospective tenants for other buildings that may have had a vacancy coming up. Alexander always had a waiting list for his buildings, and he liked it that way.

He told the owners that he did not manage other people's property, but would be interested in discussing his purchase of the property. They indicated they would think about it, but at the moment they were in the process of moving to Vero Beach, Florida (140 miles north of Coral Gables).

Alexander kept in touch with them and his eye on these 21 apartment units. He saw that they had given the management of the building to a local realtor whose office was three blocks away.

When he began to see vacancy signs appear on the property, he called the realtor and asked what they were asking and visited the property, which had declined substantially in the two years since the owners had moved to Vero Beach. There were seven vacancies in the building, so following the visit to the property Alexander did some snooping around and discovered that there were several tenants in the building that he suspected were dealing in drugs. Whatever was going on, it was driving the other tenants out of the building.

As a rental apartment property, Alexander knew that in decent shape the apartments should command a rent roll of nearly $490,000 a year based on the two-bedroom apartments, which contained 1,480 square feet of rental area at a rental of $1,800 per month. The three-bedroom apartments were just over 2,300 square feet each and would easily rent for $2,800 per month. The total square feet of rentable space consisted of 33,540 square feet. The present rent structure was considerably below these amounts, and reflected the condition of the building and the bad tenant situation there. This was clearly a combination of bad management and absentee ownership.

Alexander called the owners and told them he was aware of their vacancy factor in the building and offered to lease the entire building on a triple net basis. He would pay them $210,000 per year plus all expenses of the operation. In addition, he would give them $100,000 worth of upgrade work to the building, which he pointed out was in pretty bad shape. For this $100,000 of repairs and upgrade work, he wanted an option to purchase the property anytime within the next three years for $2,000,000. As an incentive for him to purchase the property sooner, though, he asked that the full $100,000 option sum be applied to the purchase price if he closed on the sale by the end of the second year. Of this work, Alexander anticipated that around $25,000 of it would be supplies and material, mostly paint and some carpet in the hallways. The apartments, Alexander knew, had hardwood floors, which would need refinishing. The balance of the $100,000 was labor, which Alexander had on full-time employ anyway. This was his sweat equity of $75,000 that would be his once he closed on the sale. He knew he would close by the end of the second year at the start of this transaction.

Option to Buy

The option to purchase at $2,000,000 was a fair value for the property as a rental apartment building based on the revenue that he had offered the owners. His net rent to them of $210,000 was actually a bit more than they were currently making after expenses with their present occupancy situation, and Alexander knew that it would not take him long to turn the property around.

At the end of six months Alexander had finished with the fix up of the property, gotten rid of the bad tenants, and filled the apartments with new tenants at much higher rents. He kept his new leases at one year maximum.

He contacted the owners and asked them if they would be interested in holding a first mortgage and letting him buy earlier. They responded that they would need to get at least 50 percent of the purchase price down to make that attractive to them. He said if he did that would they hold a first mortgage at 5 percent interest, payable interest only.

As interest available in banks, even long-term Certificates of Deposit were paying around 4 percent and the idea of a strong mortgage with excellent collateral would be better than that. Alexander said he would get back to them in a few months and see if he could work it out for them that way.

Sliding Mortgage

Alexander had no intention of giving them a first mortgage on the apartment complex, but he did have several other properties that were free and clear and that he had planned to put on the market. One of them, an office building, was worth around $2,300,000, which had cost him less than half that several years earlier. He had fixed it up, brought up its rent roll, and was now going to take his profit out. He decided that if he put a $1,050,000 first mortgage on the office building at 5 percent interest only with a 15-year balloon, he could easily sell the property by holding a second mortgage of $1,066,000 at 8 percent interest only. That would mean that a buyer with $184,000 (only 20 percent of the $2,300,000) could purchase the office building for 20 percent down and would have a debt service on the combined first and second mortgages of $137,780 a year.

The office building has a real NOI of $350,000. after all expenses except debt service, including a 6 percent management fee to Alexander's new management company. If the total debt service is only $137,780, this means there would be a cash flow of $221,220.

Alexander's Office Building Would be Security for the First Mortgage

Property value around	$2,300,000
First mortgage @ 5% interest only 15 year balloon	– 1,050,000
Second mortgage @ 8% interest only 15 year balloon	– 1,066,000
Down payment when Alexander sells the building	$ 184,000

The office building new buyer would have a debt service shown below:

First mortgage at 5% on the office building	$ 85,280 per year

This would go to Vero Beach as part of the purchase of the 21 units in Coral Gables

Second mortgage at 8%	$ 52,500 per year
Total debt service to investor buying this building	$ 137,780

Interest Only Debt

What Alexander has created is a soft mortgage with a very low loan to value ratio on an office building he plans to sell anyway. The low interest at 5 percent and the interest only term is way below the current market, but as Alexander will not be holding the mortgage but instead he is going to *slide* the mortgage over to the hands of the Coral Gables apartment owner. This is the same as Alexander getting 100 percent cash out of that mortgage. The low debt service also makes the sale of the office building very attractive and in a year or two Alexander will likely *slide* that mortgage to someone else in another deal.

Alexander calls the owners of the 21 units and tells them how he plans to structure the deal. He sends them photos of the new office building and after some negotiation agrees to give them a first right to purchase the office building (on which they will already hold the first mortgage), and he will give them a second mortgage for $1,200,000 to sweeten the deal. He also agrees that they can take that deal if they want right now, and all they have to do is come up with $50,000. He reminds them that he will still be giving them $1,050,000 cash when he closes on the 21 units, so they will actually have $1,000,000 net cash after all the smoke clears. Since every one of Alexander's properties is in a separate corporation, each property owner of record is someone other than Alexander himself. This is an important factor should this deal evolve to an IRS Section 1031 transaction. Each property can be dealt with as though it was coming from a different entity, even though Alexander controls each of the properties.

How the Deal Finally Closes

1. Coral Gables Sellers had agreed to take the $1,050,000 first mortgage on the office building instead of a mortgage in the same amount on the 21 units. For Alexander's company buying the 21 units, to close he will write them a check for $1,050,000, which represents the balance.

2. They also agree to purchase the office building; the seller (Alexander) will arrange financing. They will give back to Alexander $50,000 of the cash mentioned above.

3. The deal closes as a *tax free* exchange under Internal Revenue Code Section 1031. This means they do not have any capital gains tax to pay on the gain from the sale of the 21 units.

Economic Conversion

Before closing on the 21 apartments, Alexander moves forward with the final documentation of the deal. He has put up a deposit of $200,000 to the sellers of the 21 units to bind the deal, and he files condominium documents for the 21-unit building as a residential/work loft condominium. This is a form of loft apartment that is growing in popularity in many cities around the world. He knows that he will be able to easily sell these condos for $350 to $375 per square foot. The ultimate sell out for Alexander will be at least $11,739,000. ($350.00 × 33,540 square feet = $11,739,000)

His fix up cost for this final stage will cost him approximately $2,500,000 so here is how the deal looks from Alexander's point of view.

Alexander's Point of View

Ultimate gross sales from the loft condos	$11,739,000
Less cost	
Acquisition of 21 units	$ 2,000,000
Conversion cost	2,500,000
Total cost (deducted from gross sales)	4,500,000
Profit to Alexander	$ 7,239,000

Alexander accomplishes this by giving the office building to the former apartment building owners. They will pay to him, at the closing, $300,000, which comes out of the financing that is arranged to be placed on the office building following the closing.

Alexander finances the conversion to work/lofts from a local savings and loan. Alexander's total out of pocket cost is really zero.

Final Analysis for the Sellers of the 21 Unit Apartment Building

1. The owners of the 21 units exchange the apartments for the office building.

2. Financing is arranged so that they get $1,300,000 in new financing on which they have no tax to pay. The mortgage will be at 8 percent interest only for 15 years. Payment will be $104,000 per year.

3. They increase their tax basis remaining from the 21 units by $300,000, which is the benefit of the office building as compared to the value of the 21 units.

4. The owners of the office building will have a cash flow paid to them in monthly installments from Alexander's management company as shown below:

NOI	$350,000
Less debt service	104,000
Cash flow	$246,000

Alexander went slowly in this transaction and never jumped into the deal as a direct exchange. Only after the sellers had agreed to hold a mortgage for $1,050,000 at 5 percent did he realize that if he first *slid* the mortgage to the office building, then agreed to manage that for them from his new management company, the deal could easily move to a tax free exchange. Which it did.

Creative thinking can sometimes produce amazing win-win results.

CHAPTER 6

Proven Investment Strategies That Increase Equity Buildup

The goal of this chapter is:

To Give You Insider Information to Enable You to Find Properties That Allow You to Quickly Build Equity

---

This chapter is designed to illustrate the more dramatic events that can happen to your real estate investments when you are aware of their potential. One of the key factors in this is timing, which is actually a relative thing to observe. After all, when you are on the receiving side of the event, and a property you put under contract a week ago suddenly is being sought after by other investors at three times the price you will have to pay when you close, other people may view this as the luck of the draw. "How could that guy be so lucky?" They might ask.

But you will know better. It had very little to do with luck and far more to do with a careful awareness of what is going on in the community and with the forces that control when and how much values go up—or down.

I have mentioned already that in retrospect it is easy to call the way the football game will go. And yet, once you begin to see a review of the events that had an impact on real estate value (either up or down), you will begin to see that the signs of such a move were there for you to see way before the value made its move. But where were those signs, and why didn't you see them.

The truth is you likely did see them, but they did not register. For the ten millionth time let me repeat: Nothing that is caused by man, which can affect real estate values, happens quickly. The signals begin to show up early through subtle movements in the political structure of the local community. This happens with complaints from different government departments that they are underfunded, or that other departments are usurping their authority. Infighting within the governing authorities starts to show its ugly head outside the commission or councilmen's chambers. Building and zoning problems or problems within the building and zoning departments hit the newspaper. Some major employment centers or companies lay off some people and hint that there may be more to come. An outside employment center announces a possible move to the area. The governor of the state gives a press conference and announces that a major new government project has been funded for your area. New road and bridge works are being discussed. The school board says they don't need more schools so their five-year advance funds can go to other uses. And the list continues. These signs are everywhere if you look for them. Are there vacancy or no-vacancy signs around? Do businesses have NOW HIRING signs or banners across their windows? Do you suddenly complain about the heavy traffic that wasn't there last year? Or are the streets nearly empty and you thank God that there is no traffic? Think about all this. Look back over the past 30 or so Sunday front pages of the local section, or just think about what is going on around you, and I'll bet you will see most of what led up to the current prosperity, or economic gloom.

So, what do you do? You beat the newspapers and the television reporters to the punch. You start watching or listening to the source of the news. Attend local planning and zoning meetings, go to commission meetings, and attend school board meetings. Some of these may even be available on your local cable TV network. Go on the Internet and look at the published agendas for these meetings. Generally they will be available and, if not on the Internet, by mail.

Terms and Concepts You Need to Know

Many part-time investors or those new to real estate may choose to put their trust in properties that will maximize equity buildup potential instead of cash flow. Of the different ways that this can occur, the following are the most dynamic of them all, and they are so important, I call them the Four Magic Factors of Equity Growth.

The Four Magic Factors of Equity Growth

A Cooked Development
Dramatic Change in Zoning and/or Development Criteria for Approval
Tax Law Changes
Sudden Realization That Developable Sites Are Disappearing

Let's review each of these in detail.

A Cooked Development

The term "cooked" in this instance has just the opposite connotation to that of "cooked goose." The cooked development is one where the owner—often an investor who has just recently purchased the property, or at least has it in control via a binding agreement—has gone through the process to obtain approvals and "entitlements" to develop, or build, or alter the current use into something new. This new venture will likely become the basis of interest from other investors who do not have the patience to spend the time and effort to wade through the bureaucratic swamp that sometimes confronts developers of new projects.

I have seen property values climb through the roof when commission votes indicate that the majority is in favor of the project. And, just to show you, I have seen the property owners near to tears when the vote went the other way.

Many investors devote their life to bringing raw tracts of land or tired old buildings through this process to the point where new development can take place—without ever carrying through on the project themselves. There is a great deal of profit to be had this way, when the timing is right.

There are times when it looks as though the development boom will continue forever, or at least a few more years. Then the rumors start that the issuance of new housing permits is down 15 percent from the month before. Panic can spread quickly, even though no one pays attention or reads the text of the article that indicates the city in question was Chicago and it is now December and an artic snow has been falling for the past 27 days.

But whatever the reason, doubt does begin to creep into the marketplace, and for some areas of the country doubt is all it takes to slow the boom market down, perhaps even kill it altogether. When that happens, the cooked development might become as important as yesterday's oatmeal, still in the pot, but no longer appealing to any developer's appetite—at least until the market picks up again, and then only if the approvals are still valid.

Dramatic Change in Zoning and/or Development Criteria for Approval

The supply and demand of real estate is an important speed control device that may indicate how strong and how long a rising market will last. Look at some of the obvious questions whose answers will point to important directions.

How Much Developable Real Estate Is There? If the hot market is in multifamily condominiums and/or townhomes, are there areas of land at prices that make this development possibility still available? Many cities run out of this kind of land area many times over their history. When this happens, old buildings are torn down, and new ones developed. At least that used to be the trend. But lately many cities are taking advantage of the lower priced land and are buying it up themselves to turn it into parks, or simply green space to keep developers from getting their hands on that land. Major infrastructures, such as highways that snake through poorer (and cheaper land areas) also gobble up land that might have become new housing to replace tired old housing.

Then there are the changes in zoning that leave the land available for developers but not at the right zoning to allow the uses to meet the current demands of the market. Now, take note of the double-edged sword that the local officials wield when these changes are made. The land that has this direct negative impact will likely not go up in value, unless the remaining uses (if any) become attractive to developers who can no longer do what they wanted to do. On the other hand, land that has escaped the wrath of the planning and zoning officials will be even more in demand, and its value will take off like a skyrocket.

Is There a Hint There Will Be More Developable Areas Available Soon? Sometimes people in city government are aware of the economic need to sustain development in the community and act to insure that it continues. They generally do this for two basic reasons: (1) the economic benefits to the local community will continue, and (2) affordable housing (which is often a partial requirement of a major development) will insure that the city will have a place for workers and not just for the rich and retired.

Economic benefits can be many. First are the jobs that are made available for the construction side of the project. Then there is the sales side, where the real estate profession profits. Because not all sales of new housing, as an example of a category of development, go to out of town buyers, local people move from rental properties (which frees up that space for newcomers) as well as their present homes, which now enter the recycle market.

Affordable housing is slowly becoming a thing of the past, as market rate projects are more the case with developers who want to avoid the regulations that come with building affordable housing (which has local subsidy to supplement the rents the tenants cannot afford).

If there is nothing being done by the local government to help generate the right building incentives or to allow for rezoning to open urban and rural areas that are closed to new development due to the wrong kind of zoning, then the community may become stagnant for a period of time. During that time, downtown areas may slip into economic decay, and eventually there is a push to stop this nonsense and get a redevelopment plan together. It works this way.

Are political plans heading toward such redevelopment of prime development sites? In a community that is experiencing a decline of economic conditions or the rise of crime in areas of town or the county, it is up to the local authorities to take steps to encourage the redevelopment of those areas.

If this occurs, you will not automatically see a sudden improvement or even any new development for a while. It can take several years for local planners to come to agreement as to what kind of redevelopment should occur, and what may seem to be endless public debate on how things are to move forward. Politics moves very slowly, and the bureaucratic method even slower.

This means that although the right process may be working, do not jump into the foray too soon. Sit back and watch what is happening. Keep your eyes open for values to drop even more before they begin to rise. Why? Many property owners grow tired of the anticipation of change, especially when it does not happen as promised. Property owners may even stop what little repair they have been giving to old buildings (which ultimately will be torn down to make way for new development) and sell now.

Tax Law Changes

Any tax law is subject to change. This goes for any kind or category of federal taxes, state taxes, gas taxes, and local tourist or hotel taxes, and so on. Some of these laws can have a direct impact on the value of real estate in the community.

In 1986 there was a major shift in the federal income tax rules that made investment in second homes less desirable. Almost overnight this had a major impact on the entire second home market across the country. Other laws that have limitations on certain real estate–oriented deductions, such as interest on mortgages, or the amount of depreciation you can take on a rental property in any given year, can erase the small benefit that led an investor to purchase that kind of property in the first place. In some communities there are taxes against things such as hotels in certain areas of town, with the tax raised to support a convention center or other tourist activities or infrastructure. Gas tax can partially go to road and bridge construction, and so on. Each tax devised generally has a defense as to why it was introduced, and sometimes the negative side of the tax is not well thought out.

There are those in power (federal, city, state, county, and city) that think new taxes are the ultimate support of government and so are essential to the existence of political control. This may be true, but why, then, do certain taxes vary so greatly across the country. Some states have low real estate taxes, while others tax the property owner to the hilt. Some states have a state income tax, as well as high real estate taxes while others do not. Let's look at a few taxes that have negative impact on real estate value unless there is a positive side that overrides that negative effect.

Real estate ad valorem taxes (local real estate tax) that are assessed by the county tax assessor may have an annual cap on how much the county can raise the taxes for personal residences that the owner lives in (and not rents out). California was one of the first states to push for this kind of law, and it has a strong impact on the owners of such properties, but not always in a positive way. Here is how it works. Let's assume that the state in question has mandated that no country assessor can raise a person's ad valorem by more than 3 percent in any given year. In an average upscale neighborhood, the market value of the homes may be rising 10 to 20 percent per year over a long period of time. The Fort Lauderdale home owner who purchased a property 20 years ago and paid $300,000 at that time may now live in a neighborhood that is going through a renaissance where the 30-to-50-year-old homes are being removed, and million dollar plus homes going up in their place. The property owner who has kept a home for this same period of time has experienced an increase over the time, likely 60 to 75 percent increase over what it was at the time the home was first purchased. This might relate to an original ad valorem of $3,000 per year to a tax of $5,250 20 years later. But a buyer of this home at its real market price might end up with an ad valorem tax bill at the end of the year well over $30,000. Your first reaction to this is how great this is for the property owner who has kept his home for all this time. Look at the modest taxes he pays in relationship to what a buyer will pay. While that logic is sound, what is this property owner going to do? If he sells, say for $1,500,000 where is he going to buy where he can afford to pay the new taxes? This situation saves tax money while still living in the home, but is also an incentive not to sell the property.

To some degree the high capital gains tax that was in effect for a long time, only to be reduced a few years ago, served as an incentive not to sell your property. Take a profit—that's okay—but do so with a penalty of paying a ton of capital gains tax. The current capital gains rates have helped free up a lot of real estate that otherwise would not have been placed on the market. The minimum capital gain rate is presently 10 percent, and for most real estate may only be 15 percent, which is a big savings over the former rates that exceeded 35 percent in some cases. The current low rates have encouraged people to sell now, because the present savings help offset the new ad valorem tax investors may have to pay when they buy a new home. However, it is a good idea to see your accountant before you sell thinking you may have only 10 percent or 15 percent tax to pay.

Tax laws are difficult to understand or even learn about. Because of this, it is important that you not make any decisions that may trigger tax consequences without first clearing your potential obligations to the taxing authorities with your accountant. It is possible to have a sale that triggers more tax than the actual cash you get at the closing. This situation is easier to occur than you might think. For example, assume you have a substantial capital gain in a property, and at the same time have taken an accelerated depreciation schedule while owning it, and have placed a new mortgage on the property to take out some of your equity (which could have been several years ago). I will give this example some numbers, as it is a relatively common situation.

Maxwell has owned a retail commercial complex for 20 years. He paid $500,000 for it when he purchased it ($50,000 allocated to the land and $450,000 to the improvements) and took an aggressive depreciation posture (at the advice of his accountant, which worked for Maxwell, since he wanted to get the maximum cash flow out of the commercial units). Five years ago he realized that the property was worth over one million dollars, and his accountant suggested that he put a new mortgage on the property, which he did. The new mortgage was interest only for 10 years in the amount of $800,000, which Maxwell used to acquire other investment property. Because the money was a mortgage secured by the complex, Maxwell did not have to pay any tax on the funds.

Now, five years later he gets an offer to sell the property for $1,500,000 if he will let the buyer assume the existing mortgage (and the lender says okay), if Maxwell will take a beautiful sailboat worth $200,000 as part of the down payment. The buyer will throw in another $200,000 in cash, and give Maxwell a second mortgage for the balance. Maxwell has always wanted a sailboat, so, with emotions and thoughts of slipping over the waves into the sunset, the deal is made.

Then, several months following the closing, when Maxwell's accountant is preparing his income tax, the accountant learns of the deal and delivers Maxwell the bad news. What follows is a description of the bad news.

Due to Maxwell's aggressive depreciation schedule since he purchased the buildings, everything except the land has been fully depreciated in. This means that his tax basis is only the original land cost allocation of $50,000. Remember, land is not a depreciable item and remains at its purchase price (except when mined, and then it becomes a depleted asset, which is similar to a depreciated asset).

Sales price	$1,500,000
Tax basis	50,000
Capital gain	$1,450,000
Recapture of capital gain taxable at earned income rate	450,000
Balance of capital gain taxable at	$1,000,000
Net mortgage relief due to refinancing taxed at 28%	$ 800,000
Balance of capital gain taxable at 15%	$ 200,000

Because of the accelerated depreciation rate Maxwell used, all depreciation taken is taxed at his earned income rate. This year his accountant sets that at 25 percent.

Tax due on the recaptured depreciation:

$$25\% \text{ of } \$450,000 = \$112,500$$

The next $800,000 of capital gain is first taxed at a higher income rate. This is because Maxwell took this money out in refinancing before the sale.

The tax on this amount is estimated at 28%, which is	$224,000
The balance of $200,000 capital gain is taxed at 15%	$ 30,000
Total tax due from Maxwell	$ 66,500

Review the sale.

Price	$1,500,000
Buyer Gives Maxwell	
Sailboat	$ 200,000
Cash	200,000
Second mortgage	300,000
Assumes first mortgage	800,000
Balance	$1,500,000
Tax due	$ 366,500
Actual cash to Maxwell	$ 200,000
Amount Maxwell is short	$ 166,500

The lesson here is check with your accountant first, then work out the deal so that the minimum cash you get at least covers your tax bite. Remember, in nonresidential real estate, the depreciation taken can be fully recovered as earned income. Tax-free cash you take out early in the form of new mortgages can also be taxed (later when you sell) as earned income. But take special note: all tax laws are subject to change so double-check everything that you read because tomorrow even the results of this example could be interpreted with an entirely different result.

Sudden Realization That Developable Sites Are Disappearing

You would think it does not take a genus to recognize that if all the vacant lots have been built on there will be a shortage of developable land. In that instance, if you want to build anything in the area, you have to purchase an existing building, go through whatever the current local process the building department imposes to get a permit to remove the old building, plus the hassle to design something new, and obtain the necessary approvals to build the new building.

Yet, in my experience I have found that this is not always the case. In fact, rarely is it the case, since many developers seem oblivious to this fact. Take Miami, Florida, and the surrounding area as a good example. Vacant developable oceanfront sites disappeared a long time ago. From the early 1950s until the end of 1990, developers were picking up old motels that could be purchased at a value based on the NOI of that old motel. This meant that the owners of those properties had closed their eyes to the fact that developers were not buying their property as a motel, but as a vacant parcel on which they wanted to build new hotels or high-rise condominium apartments.

But events progressed, and from 1990 until 2000 the average price developers would pay per new condominium unit they could build, was around $50,000. This meant that if the site could be approved for 200 condominium apartments the developers were paying 200 × $50,000 or $10,000,000 for the site. Then suddenly there was a hold out. The seller of a large tract in North Miami beach area wanted $100,000 per unit for his 200-unit buildable tract of land. The developer argued, cried the blues, then went home and calculated his potential profit from the site. He suddenly realized that even paying $100,000 per unit he was going to make more than double his profit than he did two years earlier down the street, paying only $50,000 per unit. Why? Because prices that buyers would be willing to pay had gone up considerably. It is the effect of supply not meeting the demand. Connect that to the fact that it is evident there is no cheaper ocean front land (that words "cheap" and "expensive" are relative to what people in other areas are paying."

Two years earlier, when the developer was paying $50,000 per unit, and building costs were $125.00 per square foot, he was lucky to sell for $225.00 per square foot. That meant that his 2,000-square-foot apartment would cost him, $50,000 for the land, and $250,000 to build (2,000 square feet x $125.00 per square foot), which would total $300,000.

On the sales side he would sell for $450,000 and would make a profit of $150,000. But times had changed, and here he is, two years later, and his building cost had climbed to $150.00 per square foot, so the same apartment would cost him $100,000 for the land, and $300,000 to build, or a total of $400,000.

But he could get $325.00 per square foot in a sale, which would bring in $650,000. His profit was now $250,000 per unit.

Time has moved on and prices for land and construction and the ability of a buyer to pay more have continued to climb. Based on recent sales of oceanfront land along the Atlantic coast of Florida in late 2005 and early 2006, the price of $200,000 per unit of new condominium construction was the going norm. Then, as the oceanfront availability began to run short, these prices jumped to non-oceanfront properties as well. It started with unique one of kind sites, such as prime river front sites that had great views of the city and in the distance spectacular sunrises or sunsets or golf course expanses. This included downtown urban renewal sites as well as more remote sites surrounded by marshes or lakes.

Take a look at the following chart to see how these prices have kept pace with the demand. Take note that this is a sample of good oceanfront developments, but is not the extreme example of what people will pay. Development costs in any given area, however, vary little. Also, keep in mind that condominium prices in New York City, Paris, London, San Francisco, Naples, Florida, South Beach (Miami) Florida, and other cities around the world can exceed $2,000 per square foot—not because development cost have accelerated that much, but mostly because to build a 40-story high-rise-mixed-use residential condo and office complex (a la Trump el magnificent), you might have to acquire and tear down a major landmark building.

Ironically, the per unit land cost for small, non-high-rise condo apartment complexes with private dockage for boats (that would have ocean access without fixed bridges) in Fort Lauderdale has already exceeded $500,000 per unit.

The Changing Times of Ocean Front Condominium Sales in Fort Lauderdale Based on a 2,000-Square-Foot Apartment Unit in a Prime Oceanfront Location

	1998/1999	*2001/2003*	*2005/2006*
Land cost per unit	*$50,000*	*$100,000*	*$200,000*
Total building/sales cost per sq. ft.	$125	$160	$240
Total actual cost to build/sell	$250,000	$320,000	$480,000
Total land and building/sales cost	$300,000	$420,000	$680,000
Price sold for per sq. ft.	$225	$325	$475
Total price the unit was sold for	$450,000	$650,000	$950,000
Developer's profit	$150,000	$230,000	$270,000

Now, as I write this, in the year 2006, things have changed again and prices per unit of oceanfront land, in Fort Lauderdale would require the investor to acquire a large hotel or condominium at what would clearly be an astronomical price. But Daytona Beach, Florida, a sleepy town that once had the most hotel/motel rooms of any area in Florida suddenly began to take off. Considering that 80 percent or so of the structures in existence on the oceanfront had been built pre-1960, things were ripe for a change. Several builders had seen what was going on in areas that had already gone through the tear down and build up phase. Naples, Florida, was just about completely developed, and condominiums there currently were selling above $650 a square foot. Single-family homes that were oceanfront, in the few places that they exist, would cost several thousand dollars a square foot due to the high cost of the land.

Today developers are buying Daytona oceanfront based on the $200,000 per unit they can build. Fortunes are being made by the few who recognized that there was a land rush about to take place and who began to tie up motel after hotel at prices that seemed high, but really were not. There is the story going around here in Fort Lauderdale of an apparently very flushed (with cash) Russian who was from somewhere in the middle of Siberia and had made millions of dollars in the Soviet privatization game. He knew little or nothing about this whole "oceanfront" phenomena thing and was told by a local Palm Beach real estate broker that the best thing he could invest in would be oceanfront land. "Okay," he said with a heavy Russian accent, "show me oceanfront land I can buy, and I will do it."

The broker blushed, and she replied, "But we don't have any."

"What do you have?" he asked.

"Acres and acres of orange groves between here and Orlando. At a very good price too," she said.

"Okay, I'll buy that and build an ocean," he answered.

Oh, by the way, that isn't so unrealistic either. If you think so, drop over to Paradise Island in the Bahamas. Here is a place that is actually oceanfront, but really took off when a Russian built an ocean on top of the beach. It is an aquarium that you can walk inside of (in clear plastic tunnels), recently belittled by one in Atlanta.

But the disappearing act happens to virtually every category of property in a community, given enough time for development to first fill up, then go through its rehab periods. The key words here are "fill up." In communities where there is no realistic end to expansion, this can take a very long time. Eventually development expands so far from what was the center of attraction in the first place that there will be a move back to urban development, and what developers call "in-fill" development begins to take place. This is what happens to small, old towns that suddenly remove the tallest building in town, a five-story bank/office building, and begin to build high-rise condominiums right in the middle of town.

So what do you do? Follow the events of property value growth in South Florida. We have lots of vacant land in South Florida; all you have to do is to fly from Orlando to Miami to see it. In the entire center part of Florida, once you get a couple dozen miles south of Orlando airport, you will see nothing much but green. But get close to the Atlantic Ocean or the Gulf of Mexico, and there is a band of development that looks as though it hugs the oceanfront and barely reaches 15 miles toward the center part. That leaves nearly 100 miles of green between the two crowded bands of development.

What caused this to happen? Is it simply that everyone wanted to be within 15 miles of the beach on one side of Florida or the other? You might say that was the original attraction, especially pre-air-conditioning when summertime very far from the open water was not so pleasant. But no, this is not the reason. The center part of South Florida is pretty much a moving mass of water. Parts of it are called the Everglades; other parts are simply conservation areas, swamps, environmentally protected lands, or sugar cane land, or land that the state of Florida has been buying up in thousand-acre hunks to keep it out of the hands of developers. If none of that stopped development, the lack of utilities, roads, and other restrictions have created a natural barrier on both sides of the Florida coast that pushes development into this narrow band.

Smart money now looks for this kind of situation—growth that is channeled in absolutely definable directions with a distinct impossibility, or improbability, of going in other directions. When you find this in a community, you can yell "eureka," because you have just found what may well be your gold mine for the future.

Where Do You Look for the Best Equity Increase Potential?

The key is to look for each of these following elements. Any single element may present an opportunity for either additional cash flow or equity buildup, but when you find situations where there are several of these elements occurring at the same time, then you are more secure in moving forward.

The Key Places and Events Where Equity Growth Is a Sure Thing

Areas with Positive Impact Due to the Magic Four Factors of Equity Growth

Where There Are Underproducing Properties You Can Turn Around

When New Infrastructure with Positive Impact Potential Is on the Way

Where There Is High Employment of Middle to High Income Jobs

When There Is a Potential to Sell Off Underproducing Elements That May Result in a Bargain

When Properties Have Economic Conversion Potential

Where Growth Is Confined and Limited by Natural or Other Barriers

Areas with Positive Impact Due to the Magic Four Factors of Equity Growth

A Cooked Development: When the situation warrants your investment consideration, and there is a combination of these events occurring in the same place, one of the best kinds of development to look for is a project that is ready to go. These projects will be available in most such markets because of several reasons. The first is the logical outcome of investor-developers who put deals together, assemble land, get the zoning and other approvals, and then sell the project to the actual building developer.

The second kind of cooked development you will find is the one that is in the process of failing to move forward. Deals fail to be completed for many reasons. These circumstances can include a major shift in the market conditions that force the developer to charge a price for the product that is too high for the available buyers. Other reasons include the inability of partners to agree on certain aspects of the project, the fear of the major deep pockets of the development to put its name on a multimillion dollar construction loan, or simply the death of the major player in the project.

Whatever the reason, there will be deals like this available, somewhere in the market area. Your key is to make sure that there is a reason for this project being available, and that the market and your ability will make it a winner—for you.

Dramatic Change in Zoning and/or Development Criteria for Approval: I have already discussed how a change in zoning or development criteria can have a sudden impact on what is happening in a market. When that has a positive effect on certain kinds of development and other aspects are also apparent in the area, then this can be one of those elements that can make your wealth multiply rapidly.

All developers and investors need to stay on top of these two factors. Zoning changes and development criteria (building codes, building rules and regulations, fire codes, and so on) are all slow to be enacted. They are discussed by the local authorities for months, even years. Sometimes they even require that the proposed change or modification be placed on a ballot (often when the next pending election comes around). But keep in mind that this is not always the case, and sometimes relatively closed discussions lead to a rather swift rule change. Nonetheless, there will be some advance warning if you stay on top of this sort of thing. Get to know the head of the departments of planning, zoning, traffic, fire, building, and code enforcement. Make sure you are proactive, to learn whether anyone is even suggesting a change that can affect (either positive or negative) property values in any way. One of the soft ways that these departments start the ball rolling is to begin a study of one situation or the other to see whether there is a need for a change or implementation of some entirely new law, code, or rule. These studies can take months to plan, and even longer to accomplish, then more time to analyze. In the end the public can grow tired of hearing about all this and become lax. Then whammy, the measure is voted in by the city counsel.

Tax Law Changes: Tax law changes, once enacted (and even though they may not go into effect until a future date, say, next September), can have a swift impact. Sometimes the impact is either negative or positive because of the initial reaction to the change. It may not be until later, when the law is in effect, that the real implication of that new tax or repeal of an old tax or whatever it is, does to the economy. The lesson to learn is to stay on top of these elements. The local board of realtors and the National Association of Realtors try to keep their members informed of such pending events. However, on a local level, there are tax changes that occur that might slip past even this ever-vigilant body of professionals. A local room tax for hotels may not appear to have a negative or positive impact on anything that would effect anyone other than the tourist that has to pay it, or the hotel that may want to absorb it, either entirely or partially. But the question should be asked, what benefits come from this tax? Is it to build a new high-speed rail transport between the airport and the major tourist area, or a new convention center, or an aquarium home for displaced whales? Some of these situations, if they ever did exist, could lead you to look at the other events and places in your area that may benefit, which other people have not yet identified.

Sudden Realization that Development Sites are Disappearing: Look around and see what is slowly being eaten away. It doesn't matter whether it is a category of real estate that appeals to you, or that you ever think will appeal to you. There may be a time that it will. Or even more likely, when you see a category of real estate development using up all the available sites for that kind of development, you may want to start looking for the other events and places described in this section of this chapter that may complement that real estate. For example, in many communities one of the scarcest of all zoning is dedicated to industrial uses, perhaps because the community has removed much of this kind of land through acquisition and conversion to parks. Or these areas have been converted to urban renewal projects and made available to developers. It could be that the Department of Transportation (DOT) has taken some of the industrial land by planning new traffic ways or other public projects to take advantage of blighted (therefore lower priced land) parts of town. That's okay for that kind of developer, but what about your interest in this kind of zoning?

Whenever you see a specific category of zoning disappearing, it is a good idea to review the actual zoning code to see what it permits. Generally industrial zoning allows a wide range of uses, some of which can be a desirable use that will employ many people in high-paying jobs. It might be that the location for this facility is found only within the industrial zoning of that community. Use some creative thought here, and you may discover a real need to reintroduce this zoning to the community. It might be done by acquiring a tract of land on the outskirts of town, where the right project could be approved. Then seek a user that needs that kind of zoning, but who presents a clean environment with high paying jobs. Can you guess what would happen to a community that had closed out all its industrial area, bit by bit? They no longer have a zoning that would allow Microsoft to relocate their entire Washington State facility there?

Where There Are Underproducing Properties You Can Turn Around

If you have a talent that is useful in taking an underproducing property and turning it into a winner, then look for properties that need that special touch. Perhaps all that is needed is a restructure of the existing tenants—or perhaps a combination of that plus some tender loving care in the form of a new paint job, or other cosmetic touches. The key to turning an underproducing property into one that gives the new owner a good return on the capital invested is to understand the market. If the property in question is a commercial rental, then clearly an investor would first need to know why the property is not producing what it should. This means that before attempting to turn a property around the investor should ascertain if there is room in the market to do that. Many an investor has acquired rental property with the belief that he could make the property produce more only to find out that the property was in fact, already throwing off the most cash flow possible. Sometimes a complete overhaul of the aesthetics of the property turns away the former clients of the tenants who were comfortable with their neighborhood hangout.

This is especially important when an investor is looking at a conversion of a rental into a for sale product. The old apartment complex that stays full at $700 per month rent may not sell out as a condominium because the price point and nature of the people who live in the neighborhood are better suited to be renters instead of owners. Some urban areas have developed into ethnic centers that are made up of people who don't want to own there. They have the mentality that if they are going to buy, they will buy in a nicer neighborhood.

Taking on the prospect of changing an entire neighborhood is a difficult task, so it is important that any property that looks like a prospect as turnaround should be in a place where at least three or four of the elements discussed here are present. Having said that, if the property, your talents, and the criteria for a turnaround are met, the investment would have good potential as a successful venture.

When New Infrastructure with Positive Impact Potential Is on the Way

Remember that new infrastructure may have only negative impact during the construction period. Even when the construction phase has completed, it may still take time for the economic benefits to mature. A new bridge, as an example, that crosses over a major highway may open up areas well beyond where the bridge is installed. The impact for the immediate area may be nothing but negative for a very long time. If the highway crosses a division of two completely diverse neighborhoods, this new link between them may cause them to meld into one larger area where the better of the two decays into more of the worst of the two. This kind of impact is not unusual. As an observant investor, you can get some advance warning that this might occur by examining why the two neighborhoods are so diverse in the first place. You may discover that the reason is one neighborhood is mostly run-down rental properties, whereas on the other side of the highway the neighborhood is an upscale community of homes and townhouses with few rental properties at all. The reason might be that the highway became the barrier that stopped the run-down neighborhood from expanding to the other side. Suddenly there is a new road and a bridge that opens the floodgates for that expansion to easily occur. A community that wanted to provide a traffic way to the distant area, perhaps at the outer edge of town, might want to encourage a redevelopment of the run-down area first.

Whatever new infrastructure can be developed, it has happened in a similar way elsewhere. Before you sink your money into any property that is near where a new large hospital is to be built, check out a town that had that happen and find out how the neighborhood around the hospital fared.

A blueprint of what might happen to your area when the proposed hospital is built can give you advance clues of what should occur.

Where There Is High Employment of Middle- to High-Income Jobs

The more people earn, the greater spendable cash they have. This cash flow filters down to every business in the community and can quickly affect the value of the real estate in that area. If there is new infrastructure planned, one of the first elements you would want to know is what will that do to the cash flow of the community. In the case of the new hospital, you might be surprised to discover that the impact may not be as great as would some other smaller infrastructure. Much will depend on what it is replacing.

Nonetheless, when a high-paying employment business relocates to a community, one of the first things they take into consideration is whether the community will be able to serve the needs of those employees. With this in mind, one of the first things you would want to do is to meet with the officials of this new business. If the infrastructure is something like a major office park, and not one employer but many, pay a visit to a similar office park that is located in a community similar to the one where the new one is planned. If the new area is a small town that is not within a two-hour drive of a major city, look for that situation and go find out how the neighborhood around the park (within a half-hour drive) has evolved. Did it change? If so, what was it before?

When There Is a Potential to Sell Off Underproducing Elements That May Result in a Bargain

A shopping center, as an example, may have several out-parcels that have never been developed. Or there may be a tenant on a long-term lease that brings down the overall yield of the center. If a new buyer of this center can sell off these underproducing elements, it may be possible to turn the balance of the property into an attractive investment with strong cash flow.

In the situation, where there are tenants in control over parts of a commercial development, like an office park or warehouse complex, selling some of the better locations to the existing tenants may reduce the balance of the acquisition to the point where the yield on what is purchased is a bargain.

Take the West Mount Office Campus that was developed as a high tech rental complex. It consisted of 800,000 square feet of total rental area contained in 20 separate buildings that ranged from 30,000 square feet to 50,000 square feet. The campus was owned by a real estate investment Trust, which wanted to sell it and had put it on the market at a price that would provide a cash flow return to an investor of around 7.5 percent of a down payment of $24,000,000. The ultimate buyer spent a couple of weeks going over the rent roll and ascertained that there were five buildings that had a total of 260,000 square feet and were below the average cash flow per square foot. It turned out that these were also five of the first eight buildings constructed in the complex, and the majority of each building was occupied by one single tenant.

With the seller's blessing, this buyer contacted these majority tenants in each of these five buildings and ended up obtaining a commitment from each of them to buy their respective buildings. Because the buildings were some of the best located ones in the campus, and because the tenants had no intent of moving, the new buyer was able to sell them at a handsome per square foot profit. The resulting sale reduced the overall price the buyer had to pay for the remaining 15 buildings. Because the five sold were among the oldest in the campus, and historically required an above-average maintenance and replacement budget, the cash flow return on the down payment was increased to over 9 percent before income taxes.

On a small scale, to sell off underproducing elements of a property can have even greater positive impact on the cash flow. The conversion of a strip mall into condominium office and shop space need not result in the sale of all the space. It may be possible and attractive for the converter to sell only enough space as condominiums as necessary to end up with a bargain in the balance of space. This tactic can have several very positive results for the center, too. By being selective as to whom and what kind of user the developer sells to, the center can be "programmed" so that it caters to a very specific nature of clientele. Because owners tend to take better care of their property than the average tenant does, a high level of maintenance can be had at a reduced cost to the developer who has retained ownership of the key locations in the center, which he then rents out at a higher square foot rental than would otherwise be possible.

The conversion of the center into commercial condominiums would allow for a general upgrade of the property, and a windfall profit to the investor.

When Properties Have Economic Conversion Potential

Economic conversions that fill a need in a community are generally very successful. The best thing about them is that the buyer of the base property can usually get a good buy. This occurs because the property is currently underperforming, usually also somewhat distressed and is owned by a motivated seller. As I have indicated before, the key to any economic conversion is to know what the current zoning will allow, and also to ascertain whether there is another zoning category that the planning department would support as a possible candidate for rezoning. Never walk away from a property because it is not zoned as you need it. Always find out whether it is possible to rezone the property. If you elect to request a rezoning, you will need a minimum of 60 days, and perhaps longer, depending on how often the local zoning authorities meet and what they will require from you. You can anticipate that you will need to illustrate exactly what you plan to do, and to be able to demonstrate that the change of use from its current situation will not adversely burden the tax payer due to the rising need for additional community services (roadways, fire and police, schools and so on). Because of the time involved, it is not wise to contract to purchase the property without a provision that would allow you to walk away from the deal if you are not approved for the needed zoning.

Forward vision is necessary when contemplating a conversion of a property to another use. The investors who are good at this task have the ability to look at a run-down motel and see a boutique antique center, or condominium offices, or an upscale medical center. Through careful review of the zoning, you should get some ideas as to what use would be good for the area, while at the same time attracting tenants and or buyers of the end product.

After you have identified several kinds of uses that you believe would work, drive around town (or other towns too) and look at properties that are dedicated to those same uses. This will give you an idea about how that use might be adapted to the buildings at the present site under consideration. If you can use the existing buildings, you may be way ahead of the game as to cost and time between the signing of the purchase agreement and the opening of the new venture.

Where Growth Is Confined and Limited by Natural or Other Barriers

As I have indicated earlier, when there are geographical or other barriers that force the flow of development in predictable and concentrated directions, the investor has an easier time selecting locations that will increase in value. Barriers can be anything that blocks the expansion or flow of development. Limited-access highways are good examples of man-made barriers, as are railroads that tend to have limited crossing points, but these are often bridged so while they are effective in dividing a community, they may not be absolute deterrents to the continued migration of development.

Rivers, lakes, oceans, mountains, deserts, and government-controlled parklands or wilderness represent both predominant barriers as well as desirable amenities to the real estate that borders them. Development itself can become a barrier to other kinds of development, and large areas that are dedicated to industrial use generally become islands surrounded by different kinds of development, each evolving into a gated community designed to isolate itself from the others.

Rural communities that are not situated close to a metropolitan area tend to move along existing traffic ways that link more distant cities. As the development along these roadways begins to thicken, newer highway systems that bypass the small communities in between the metropolitan centers carry development into new territories. It is a good idea, then, to pay close attention to the long-range plans of the interstate highway system. Many new subdivisions or employment centers have been developed along these new, unclogged traffic arteries. The time to consider investing in areas that will be benefited by the removal of a barrier is before the new road is completed. But don't worry if you are not the first in line. Most people don't know the road is coming until it is built anyway.

Barriers and the removal of barriers are both real-life conditions that can shape the value of real estate. But sometimes the barrier is not visible. Invisible barriers and their removal can become absolute gold mines to the perceptive real estate investor.

Who would have thought that Las Vegas, Nevada, would ever develop to its present dynamic impact on a patch of desert between Albuquerque and San Francisco. Someone had a vision that took hold, and in a relatively short period of time it became one of the fastest-growth areas in the United States. The unseen barrier was removed by the advent of airconditioning.

CHAPTER 7

Tips on How to Balance Cash Flow and Equity Buildup to Best Fulfill Your Investment Goals

The goal of this chapter is:

Discover How to Blend Cash Flow and Equity Buildup

I began this book with the promise that my techniques, tips, and traps would illustrate how to maximize the benefits from both cash flow and equity buildup. How each investor relates to these elements will depend a great deal, on the investor's talent and the goals that need to be addressed. Two traps in this last sentence confound many investors and become major pitfalls that need to be overcome. Those two traps are the investor's talent and the goals on which those talents need to be focused.

The first of these two elements, the investor's talent, should be seen as a sapling that needs to be fertilized and nurtured. Just as a towering pine did not start out that way, to be a successful real estate investor requires learning and practice with well-defined intermediate goals that are realistic, measurable with a timetable, and directed to a tangible and worthy objective.

This book is part of that learning process, but that talent and the self-confidence that will grow with it cannot occur from the benefit of this book alone. This maturing process requires a continued effort by investors on the elements that expand their investment talents. That effort will be a process of ascertaining what they need to know, then fine tuning their existing talents by developing the future vision that enables the investor to see what is not there. Real estate is, after all, a matter of taking something that you can see and turning it into something that you can define and describe (often just to yourself), but which does not yet exist.

The learning process of any real estate investor is also a building phase where a person discovers that there are several different kinds of people in the immediate investment circle. These are the home-team players, the advisors and mentors, positive people and negative people.

The home-team players are the people for whom all this is about. Some of these people may not have arrived on the scene, so room has to be kept open for them, and their, perhaps, particular needs and future goals. The home-team players are the family, the special friends, and, of course, the investor.

There will be the advisors and mentors that help lead the investor down the right path. That path may not always be the right one because not all investors are able to confide or to fully describe in the goals that they wish to attain and fulfill. However, eventually the investors will discover for themselves, by examples of the paths their advisors and mentors have followed, which is the right one for them. Not all of the advisors and mentors will stay on the team. Some of them will become envious of their student or jealous of the pupil's success and will no longer be trustworthy. The art of learning which person will be a positive influence in your life is essential to maximize your potential for success in any endeavor.

In fact, much of a person's business life is segmenting people into one of two categories: the positive thinkers and the negative thinkers. Negative thinkers are everywhere. You already know some, I am sure, although you may not have realized the negative impact that they have on you. They may appear charming, even be charming, but not sincere, and their ultimate desire is to thwart your every move and to make sure that whatever success you have will be less than their own success. The odd thing about these people is that they may actually be unaware of their negative nature. Alternatively, they may be very aware of it and are cunning in the way that they deal with you. These people cannot be totally avoided, nor should they be. It is far better to know which category they are in. Even snakes have their place in the business world, and once you recognize who they are, you can deal with them without having to trust them.

The positive people are also everywhere, only they may not congregate around you. The positive person may see you as a negative person because of the negative people you hang out with. You see, the negative people will seek you out, so you only have to stand still for a while for them to find you. The positive people require that you must seek them out. Fortunately, they do not hide from you, and they do not pretend not to be a positive person. Quite the contrary, they generally exude a glowing positive aura. In addition, best of all, they hang out with other positive people. If you want to join that club, you will quickly discover that their membership rules are simple. You must be positive and most importantly, you must begin to distance yourself from the negative people that surround you.

The other trap that was contained in that earlier sentence was the requirement to establish strong goals on which the investor needs to focus. Most people do not know how to properly and effectively establish goals. Without sound goals, it is easy for a person to follow the wrong path. Not only is this time consuming, it can become far more difficult to reorient oneself back to the proper pathway. Let me help you effectively set goals through a very easy process. First, however, take a moment to read the following definition of what I call Effective Goals.

An effective goal, oriented to any task, is to remember that the goals are the stepping-stones for an end objective. People tend to think of a goal as the actual result or the final objective, as if the desire to play football for a specific professional team were the goal. It is clearly the objective, but the goal, or actually the series of goals, are the steps that get you through all the stages from a point in time until you are talented enough to be chosen as a player, which is the objective.

These steps are full of individual proactive tasks that begin as you learn to play football (or establish a real estate comfort zone) and move you toward the objective of being selected in the NFL draft (or closing on your first real estate investment).

Each task, or interim goal, should require you to do something. It should have a measure to it, have a timetable, and be directed toward the ultimate objective. A measure is important and separate from the timetable. The measure is so you know where you are in the process of a specific interim goal. There is one measure that should be avoided. That is money. It is one thing to have the objective to become financially independent. That is an attainable goal. It is far different to have an objective that is "to be rich," because that is a matter of relative consequence. I never met a "rich" person who had stopped trying to get more.

The timetable aspect is how much time you have provided for yourself to meet that goal so you can move on to the next interim step. In retrospect, there should be no gaps between the interim steps, and they should not be so strictly planned that there is no opportunity to make sudden, on the spot changes in the plans. This is particularly important when these interim steps deal with other people. Instant decisions need to be made when things move more quickly than anticipated or drag to a halt because of personality conflicts.

To effectively establish your goals, try the following exercise. For one week, tell yourself, in silent thought, that at the end of that week you are going to write down three things. These three things will be (1) Vision, (2) First five intermediate steps, and (3) Timetable of these first five intermediate steps.

The vision is what you see that you have accomplished by the end of a period between 5 to 10 years from now. This is a vision where you can see yourself and other members of your home-team at end of this specific objective. You will see how you and they live, what kind of lifestyle they have, and what you do. You might be owner-operator of your own hotel, or chef of your own restaurant. You might be retired, living on your yacht in the Mediterranean, or living in a mountain chateau in Colorado teaching your grandchildren how to ski. Whatever you see should be the result of your attaining a goal by that period.

The first five intermediate steps will be the five most important things you must do that will take you from the present to that vision. These steps are what move you from point to point along the way to that distant objective. This objective is not the end of your life; it is, as it will turn out, simply another interim step in the progress of things. In reality, there will be more than five intermediate steps, but right now just think of the basic steps that you need to accomplish. It is important now that you look for steps that require you to grow your talents along the way. These steps must fit in the puzzle in one direction only. The first step should be directed toward the other four, but to get to the Vision, all five steps need to be taken in the order that you initially see them. If you are capable of reaching step five by the time you have completed step three, you can, later on, omit step four, but equally, if when you reach three you might need to add five more to continue moving forward.

Think about that Vision. What do you need to know and do to reach it. Get a better job? Learn a new profession? Begin to form a comfort zone?

You will just think about these things every day, during a time of the day or night when you can do this uninterrupted for at least half an hour. At the end of the week, you will sit down and write what you see in the Vision. Try to be as detailed as you can about what you see. Are you married? Are there children? Are you ready to be successful?

Then write down the first five intermediate steps in the order as you believe them to be. The first step should be attainable within three months, the others at the pace you will now set. The last factor in this objective-oriented exercise is to put a complete timetable to the first five intermediate steps. As you go from step one, put a period of time that it will take you to complete step one, then start step two, and so on. What you will leave out in this process will be what other things you are doing that are productive toward this final goal, the Vision. In other words, if your final Vision is that 10 years from now you are a successful heart surgeon, the five steps might have been:

1. Be accepted at Harvard Medical School

2. Graduate in the top 5 percent of your class

3. Intern at a Cleveland Clinic Hospital

4. Train under the foremost heart surgeons in the country

5. Pioneer a new method of heart surgery

The individual day-to-day elements that allow you to advance from now to these five intermediate steps would be worked out later. They will surely include:

1. Do what is necessary to be accepted at Harvard Medical School

2. Develop an effective study routine that enables you to be a top student

3. Plan a course of study that will help you be accepted at a hospital of your choosing

4. Know that your choice will allow you to train with the best

Once written down your timetable, the five intermediate steps, and the Vision will become the initial goal that you will have effectively established. It will be critical for you to monitor the measure of time it takes you to reach each of these five intermediate steps. It will be likely that by the time you get to step two that you will realize that your timetable was unrealistic, and you will need to adjust it.

As you undertake the process, you will build more intermediate steps to keep you on the right path, and as close to your timetable as possible. Every step should be forward, in a positive way. A salesman would, for example, set, as a goal for the outcome of an important meeting with a new prospective client "to make a bonding contact" rather than "make the sale." How you perceive the results is important. To make a bonding contact establishes far more than just making a sale. Even smaller elements to this process that advance the "bonding" part of this goal would be "to be five minutes early for the meeting." Each of these elements is positive, obvious, and connected. By making these conscious interim goals, you reinforce your own positive nature. By acknowledging to yourself that you know it is important to be early to an appointment, your effort to achieve that goal propels you forward. When you show up early, and act out your next interim steps (to show self-confidence, be pleasant, complimentary, and socially to the point), you start to feel good about yourself, and you quickly reach the "make a bonding contact" stage.

Terms and Concepts You Need to Know

The Unique Character of Real Estate
Community Active

Review these two elements.

The Unique Character of Real Estate

Real estate is a hands and eyes on type of investment. It is one of the only investment forms that cannot be prepackaged and sold as a commodity. While a portfolio of hotels may be purchased as an investment package, each of those hotels is different in many ways from any other hotel in the portfolio or in the world. For better or worse, in every tract of land, rental apartment building, or even condominium in a building of 500 seemingly identical units, there is something different about each one.

This means that you have an opportunity to create an advantage over other investors if you know what that difference is. If you think for a moment about your neighborhood, most people who live in a subdivision, for example, do not really know much about it. Are all the lots the same size? When were the homes built? Who lives a block away? What did they pay for their home or apartment? All simple questions that begin to make sense when you are attempting to get a feel for this area, which might become your comfort zone.

I promise you that with a little effort in a few months you can become one of the most informed people in town about this area you have chosen to make as your investment zone. As an expert on the area, you will easily see opportunities. So easily in fact that you may question are they really an opportunity.

Community Active

Because real estate is unique, the more you are connected to the community the easier it will be for you to build your knowledge of that community. In the long haul, it will be the neighborhoods in your comfort zone that will put the cash flow in your bank account and build equity for your financial independence. So, be prepared to give something back to this community. Get involved in local events, join a service-oriented club, become involved with self-help organizations, such as Toastmasters International, or take yoga classes, and so on.

From my own experience, I can tell you that giving back to what makes you a success is one of the best things you can do. It allows you to help others, while giving you both status and self-confidence.

Seven Tips on Balancing Cash Flow and Equity Buildup

Comfort Zone Management

Every real estate investor needs to have at least one comfort zone. I have stressed this in almost every chapter of this book. This geographic area need not be fixed to one part of town or even any single town. It can expand as your needs and real estate appetite expands. However, the level of knowledge about each area should encompass the same knowledge. An in-depth understanding of the local zoning ordinances and building codes is an absolute essential. And because these ordinances and codes may vary between cities, your ability to make meaningful comparisons (and avoid the green grass syndrome), will depend on that knowledge.

Management of the comfort zone needs careful planning. The material you gather in the quest for knowledge about this geographic area should be maintained in a neat and orderly way, to insure that when you need to check something you have quick access to it. Fortunately, in this Internet-driven world, much of the data you need can be found quickly from your own computer. If you do not have a computer, then establish this as your next interim goal. You can acquire an inexpensive computer for several hundred dollars that will carry you through until you can upgrade it.

Learning to navigate the Web can be intimidating at first, so the best way to learn how to access the information you need will be to pay a visit to the different city departments to make sure that (1) their data is available on the Internet, (2) that you obtain their direct web address, and (3) that you have someone there walk you through the steps to obtain the data you need.

The important departments are listed below:

The Tax Assessor's Office: This is one of the most important departments in local county government for the real estate investor. You will find a wealth of information about every piece of real estate in the county. The data contained may include the property's legal address, the present owner's name (and mailing address and sometimes phone number), when they purchased the property, what they paid for it, the present tax assessed value (of both land and buildings), the present ad valorem tax due, the former owner, additions to buildings, and when they were constructed. Once you have an owner's name, you can search that person or entity and find out every piece of property (in that county) that entity owns, and when they acquired it.

The Planning and Zoning Department: This department may be combined with the building department or separate from it. You need to check that out, and ultimately you will find that virtually every zoning ordinance will be at your fingertips. Zoning ordinances tell you what you can put on a property and need to be read from top to bottom to obtain a complete understanding of what can go where. Building codes are a separate issue and cover all the various elements of how things can be constructed.

There will be a direct connection between the building codes and the zoning ordinances, so make sure that you have a good understanding of the use and the building aspects that relate to it. If your investment category tends to be commercial in nature, you will need to pay careful attention to parking requirements, set backs, and fire codes.

A well-managed comfort zone will enable you to make fast decisions about potential opportunities that you come across. Many prospective investors fail to act in a timely manner and miss such opportunities. The key is to see the potential, then as quickly as possible tie up the property. You can make a careful inspection and analysis of the property once you have it under contract during your due diligence period.

Good Accounting Advice

Good accountants are not hard to find. The key to using their advice is to make sure that they understand your objectives. Left to their own perception of what you want, they can produce good advice for the wrong objective and bad advice for your desired objective. Discuss that objective with your accountants and ask if they have any suggestions or tips that can help you maximize the cash flow or equity buildup. You may discover that new tax law changes have opened some doors to new techniques that will be helpful to you.

Good Legal Advice

Just like your accountant, your lawyer should know your objectives. Many lawyers like to play devil's advocate about this and may sound as though they are trying to talk you out of that objective. Play along with them, they may actually see something you have overlooked, and your end objective may need to be fine-tuned or even changed.

Some lawyers like to make decisions for you. How you deal with your lawyers is up to you, of course, but it is important that they advise you in procedures as they pertain to legal matters. Contracts, leases, and legal notices, and anything that pertains to those elements of your business should be cleared with your lawyer before you enter into them. Laws change, and what was good 15 years ago may not be the correct procedure now.

The dialog you have with your lawyer should give you a clear understanding of the potential consequences of any legal step you may make. But make sure your lawyer knows the objectives you plan for, and your timetable. If the lawyer has any problems or objections with either of those elements, and has no valid reason for that, you may need to find another lawyer.

Home-Team Goals

Before you decide to implement a plan that is designed to maximize cash flow instead of equity buildup, you need to make sure that the home team agrees with that plan. Your partners, family members, or other associates that are directly involved in your investments should know and agree with your objectives. Nothing will get you off track quicker than having a property manager who thinks that the plan is to maximize equity build up when your accountant is going in the direction of maximum cash flow.

Plan Property Improvements

If you intend to improve a property at all, the plan for those improvements should begin before you close on the property. It is important that the plan be chronologically staged, so that new elements do not have to be undone because they are in the way for other elements. One of the important ingredients of improvements is the landscaping around buildings and property. Many cities have programs that not only encourage landscaping, but even offer free plants to property owners. Building a tree canopy in a city is an important feature for the entire community, and you may be able to obtain many trees at little or no cost from these programs. Contact the building department, and ask to whom you can talk about such a program.

Refine Leases

Your lawyer can provide you with a lease that covers virtually every potential roadblock or legal difficult that can arise. But sometimes there is something unique about a tenant that can present a future problem that the lawyer overlooked. You may, unfortunately, discover this problem when it occurs. Learn from that lesson, and make sure that your leases reflect that new knowledge so that you avoid complications in the future.

As you expand your rental properties, you can also avoid potential unknown legal problems by talking to other property owners who may have a tenant that is in the same business as one that is new to you. They may have already discovered that unique problem, and you can adjust your lease before signing it.

Timetables

Management should be by timetable. By this, I mean that you should have a schedule for all the events that need to be attended to: rent collection, mailing of notices of late rent, and swift enforcement of tenant violations. Tenants who see other tenants getting away with even the most minute lease violation can be tempted to do the same, and before you know it, you have a mutiny on your hands.

Ella's Balancing Act between
Equity Buildup and Cash Flow

This is a case study comparison of balancing the benefits of a real estate investment between maximum equity buildup and maximum cash flow. Property Number Two, described in Chapter 2, is shown below. It will be the basis for this case study.

Ella has been investing in real estate for seven years and has bought and sold four residential properties during this time. Her first property was a battered duplex where each side of this two-unit complex was a three-bedroom three-bath apartment. She lucked out when she discovered that the zoning would actually allow four units on the same lot, so as she was fixing up the place she remodeled the property into four units that consisted of two two-bedroom two-bath units and two one-bedroom apartments with a small kitchen and a bath. In doing this, she did away with the double car garage that was situated between the two original units.

Her profit from this greatly improved income property allowed her to continue with the same kind of investments, always looking for something that was underdeveloped for the zoning of the lot.

By the time she closed on her fourth property, she was ready to tackle something new. She had made a lot of good contacts in the building trades and building furnishing businesses, and wanted to find a small strip store building where she could bring in, as tenants, some of these new friends and have a small one-stop center for people like her who were fixing up properties for resale.

She learned of the property offering number two, and although it was only six commercial units, she believed she could divide them into twelve small locations for the unique center that she wanted to make. She knew that small retail spaces, when they work, bring in top dollar in rentals. She was counting on the fact that each of her prospective tenants would not compete with each other, and would, she believed, complement each other. This could create a big draw to the center and result in a win win situation for everyone.

The asking price of the center was $1,700,000.

Property Information: Six commercial units built in 1964. Zoned CB-1 (limited commercial use). Each unit consists of 1,250 rental square feet of area, and each space has its own central a/c unit. Gross rental area is 7,500 square feet. The physical size of each unit is appx. $17' \times 75'$.

Ella studied the current rental situation. Since the building had originally come on the market, hurricanes Katrina and Wilma had done substantial damage to the building. Five of the airconditioning units had been blown off the building, and the roof had some damage as well. There was water damage from the openings in the roof (where the AC units had been), and all but one tenant had moved out. The owner's insurance had agreed to cover all the repairs except for the $10,000 deductible. Ella knew that all of this was a windfall for her because the one tenant who had stayed only had a few months left on his lease.

She had one of her carpenters give her an estimate for the changes in the walls of the building to open it up into an easy flow of space for each of the twelve spaces she wanted to create.

The cost estimate came in at $115,000, and that included a finished product. The owner, through his insurance proceeds, had included in his work putting a fresh coat of paint inside and out, and resealing the parking lot. This was perfect, Ella thought, she wanted the building to look as new as possible when the grand opening took place.

Her proforma for the income and expenses was as follows:

Ella's Do-It-Yourself Center Proforma

Available for rent would be: 12 retail/service spaces, each of which was approximately 625 square feet. Her estimated base rent for each space was $1,300 per month, plus CAM of $300 per space and a Common Advertising budget of $200 per space:

Total base rent potential per year	$187,200
CAM (included all expenses and reserve)	43,200
Advertising budget	28,800

As the CAM and the advertising budget took care of all the expenses, Ella's net operating income would be the same as the base rent collected, presuming she had 100 percent occupancy.

Her projected NOI $187,200

To purchase the property, she had saved a total of $300,000 from each of the four earlier developments. Her objective with the Ella Do it Yourself Center was to hold onto this as a long-term investment and get it into a free and clear situation as quickly as possible. She projected, however, that she might not be 100 percent rented all the time, so she wanted to build in some safety valves in the investment. Therefore, she introduced a vacancy factor of 10 percent in her proforma, which reduced her NOI from $187,200, by $18,720, a year, down to $168,480.

Satisfied with her calculations, she began to negotiate to purchase the property. As there was no debt on the property, she first tried to get the seller to hold a new first mortgage, but although he indicated he would hold some paper, he needed to get at least 50 percent of the sale proceeds in cash.

Ella went to a bank she did business with and discovered that if she could reach 95 percent of her rent roll projection they would lend her 80 percent of the value of the property based on an 8 CAP of that NOI projection.

This was good news for Ella and in fact better than she had hoped. While she had, in her own mind, taken a 10 percent vacancy factor, the bank was prepared to swing the loan based on a 5 percent deduction. Using her gross rent projection of $187,200, a 95 percent of that rent roll gave her an NOI of $177,840. To CAP that at 9 percent meant the lender would value the building at $1,976,000 (NOI of $11,840 divided by .09 = $1,976,000). As the lender had said they would lend her 80 percent of the building value, the most they would lend would be $1,580,500. Ella was convinced this would work.

She then went to the seller and asked him if he would give her a break in the price if she gave him all cash at closing. He did not answer her right then, saying that he would simply consider doing something.

Ella has $300,000 in the bank, and she is comfortable that her total new construction and fix up will cost her $115,000 plus possible other costs of $50,000 for design plans, interest carry, loan origination costs, and the like. She calculated that her workmen could be working at the same time the insurance-covered repairs would take place. This would speed things up, which Ella was not sure was good for her. Her next step was to tie up the property, then get tenants for the space while she controlled the building.

She offered the owner $1,500,000.00 for the building, subject to the repairs that were covered by the insurance and the painting and sealing of the parking lot. She wanted 90 days of due diligence to get her plans in order and for the repair work to be completed. In her offer, she included that during the repair work, if the seller approved her plans, she would pay additional work to be done during that period.

The owner came back with a counter offer of $1,600,000 and Ella agreed that she would pay that sum, but only if the seller would hold a second mortgage on her current home (her more recent duplex conversion to 4 units) in the amount of $250,000 at interest only for five years. She would pay interest at the highest rate being paid each year by local savings and loan associations on certificates of deposit that are for a term of more than 12 months. The current such interest was 4.5 percent per year.

Because she was giving the seller a mortgage on another property, she knew that her lender would not mind, whereas if it had been a second mortgage on the commercial building the lender would not agree to that much leverage as her total loans to value ratio would exceed their lending criteria.

Now with a due diligence period of 90 days, Ella had her architect draw some quick renderings (artist sketches of what the remodeled building would look like) and began making her rounds to her friends in the building, decorating, and remodeling trades.

Everyone loved the project, and she ended up with 100 percent reservations that included a deposit. She was off and running.

Now all she had to do was to structure the deal so that it would maximize her desired objective, to build equity toward being free and clear as fast as possible. Let us review the financial parts of the deal:

Agreed to price	$1,600,000
Cost of remodeling	115,000
Miscellaneous costs	50,000
Total costs	$1,765,000
Less	
Second mortgage credit on her home	$ 250,000
Balance	$1,515,000

This meant that if she took only $1,515,000 loan from the bank, she would actually get back the money she had advanced of $115,000 and $50,000 out of the loan proceeds. The seller would get his $1,600,000 less the $250,000 or $1,350,000, and Ella would pay interest to the seller for five years at around 4.5 percent interest per year.

Let us recap all of this:

1. Ella advances the funds for the work on the building $115,000
2. She also spends the other costs amount she budgeted for   50,000
3. At closing the seller gets cash in the amount of $1,350,000
4. The seller also gets a second mortgage from Ella   250,000
5. The seller is fully satisfied thus far $1,600,000
6. The bank puts a first mortgage on the remodeled building $1,515,000
7. Less what Ella gets $115,000 + $50,000   165,000
8. Seller gets the balance $1,350,000

Ella meets her NOI estimate of $187,200 because she is 100 percent full. She deducts the 10 percent possible vacancy factor as she did earlier to arrive at an amount she plans to dedicate to her debt service. That amount is $168,480. Remember, she actually has more, as she is still setting aside $18,720 a year.

The first mortgage lender wants 6.25 percent interest on his mortgage and will let that be an interest only payment for 15 years with a balloon payment at the end of that time. Ella agrees to this, only if she can prepay principal anytime to reduce the outstanding balance. The lender agrees as this is also reducing the lender's risk in this mortgage.

Since her first mortgage is in the amount of $1,515,000, her fixed payment of interest for 10 years will be 6.25 percent of the outstanding balance. If there is no principal payment, she will owe, $7,890.63 per month, which equals $94,687.56 per year.

She anticipates the second mortgage will cost her $11,250 a year or $937.50 per month, which is 4.5 percent of the $250,000 the seller of the commercial building took as part of his deal. There is no principal due for five years, so Ella plans to worry about that later.

These two interest only payments give Ella a debt service of $8,828.13 per month. ($7,890.63 + $937.50) or a total for the year of $105,937.50. Since she has dedicated at least $168,480 to her debt service, she decides to pay to the first mortgage lender an extra $62,542,50, which brings her actual debt service to:

First mortgage $62,942.50 + $94,687.56, which equals $157,630.00 for the year.

This payment amount is equal to 10.405 constant rate ($157,630 divided by the original debt of $1,515,000). A quick check of the constant rate table will indicate that if Ella kept paying this amount for 15 years she will more than pay off this sum. In essence she paid interest only payments of $94,687.56 a year for 15 years which totals $1,420,313, and still owes the full amount of $1,515,000, which is a grand total of $2,935,313 (already paid plus what she still owes). Instead, she pays $157,630 for 14.5 years (about), which is a total, paid of $2,285,635 and has fully paid off the bank its $1,515,000.

As her objective was to retire all the debt on the center as fast as possible, it would not take much additional cash to cut the time down to 10 or 11 years. She should be able to anticipate additional increases in rent along the way. I have shown you what cost of living alone can do to the added value of a property due to additional cash flow. A quick projection of Ella's financial situation in 11 years with a simple increase of the cost of living at 3 percent would show that she should easily have a NOI of 133 percent above the current one. If she is taking in $187,200 in cash flow today, by the start of the twelfth year she should have $248,976 in cash flow. Keep in mind in this study we assume that CAM keeps up with all the operating costs of the property, so collected base rent is really her NOI.

At the end of 11 years, with, as I have mentioned, a modest boost in debt payments which she surely could handle, the property would be free and clear of all debt. Her cash flow at that time is $248,976. At a 9 percent CAP the value of the property would be $2,766,400 (NOI of $248,976 divided by the 9% CAP rate = $2,766,400).

There are still other benefits that Ella enjoys. She has some tax shelter, she may even get some additional breaks in the price she pays to her tenants for their services when she remodels her next property.

It is likely that prior to the end of the fifth year, she will have sold her existing home (a four-unit redo) and let the new owner have the benefit of the low interest rate. Or, if she does it soon enough, she might have included a provision in that mortgage that allows her to slide the mortgage to another property as security. That way then, she still retains the use of that $250,000 at a very low rate.

You benefit from OPM when you can let other people pay off or carry that debt for you. As long as you can earn more on your capital than the cost of OPM, you win.

Eight Traps You Need to Avoid

A trap differs from a roadblock in one distinct way. The trap tends to lure you into its grasp. It is the pioneering spirit of being the first developer in town to turn the slum into a beautiful upscale community, or to own the villa overlooking the vast expanses of the Marsi Mara in Kenya. It is so cheap how can you pass it up? Or the tenant who wants to rent your empty store and body piercing or not, you need the rent. Each of the following traps has something that can be appealing, which can turn out to bite you.

The roadblock, on the other hand is quite the opposite. It does not lure you, instead it tries to turn you away. Both situations can be bad for you if you get bogged down trying to get around it or turn it into a win win situation.

Win win situations that begin as a nightmare do happen, but it is so much easier to go with the flow. Deal with traps by turning your back on the temptation, even when you know it is bad for you. Some of you will yield to that temptation and write an overly friendly lease to your sister-in-law's cute niece from another marriage.

Roadblocks that stand in the way of you and your objective need to be met head on. But this first contact should be without confrontation. Never be in a rush when a roadblock is right in front of you. Ascertain if it is really a roadblock or simply a detour. If the situation is only temporary and you have the time, then sit back and let it work itself out. If you do not have the time to wait, then examine the alternatives. First, find out if there are any. If not then your fail-safe decision might be to retreat and take another direction to another objective.

Review each of these eight traps in detail.

Urban Renewal

Greener Grass Strikes at Home

Bad Tenant Mix

Overly Friendly Leases

Cutting Down on Maintenance

Under Insured

Management by Default

Code Violations

Urban Renewal

Never be the first to do urban renewal in any urban area. Pioneering this kind of development can be filled with mistakes, so let someone else make those mistakes. You can learn a lot by sitting on the sideline. If the first project is a success, there will be room for more later on. Some urban renewal projects get bogged down, however, so stay on the sideline for a while and marvel at the lessons you are learning at another's expenses.

Greener Grass Strikes at Home

It is easy to see how the Green Grass Syndrome can strike you when you are visiting some beautiful far off land for the first time. Everything is different and can be so appealing that many an investor has ended up owning a very bad dream of a property because he did not know how to do due diligence. However, green grass can grow across the street from a building you own, simply because that side of the street is in another town, or even county and the rules and regulations are greatly different. I own a strip office/retail building in Fort Lauderdale, and two doors away the city boundary ends, and another city begins. I should have known exactly where that division of cities was, but I got carried away with green grass fever and nearly purchased a property when I saw the for sale sign go up. Fortunately, my contracts have a due diligence period, and my lawyer noticed that the legal address for the property on the deed was the city of Oakland Park, Florida. A check of the zoning for that city showed that what I had intended on doing with that building was not allowed.

Bad Tenant Mix

A property that has a bad tenant mix needs to be avoided unless the leases are such that cleaning up that situation can be accomplished quickly. If the offensive tenants have long-term leases, or options to renew, it can be very difficult to get rid of them.

When this situation presents itself, you must audit all the leases of the property and protect yourself against any potential that the tenant may have a different lease or addendum to his or her lease that is different from what the owner of the building gives to you during your due diligence period. It could be that the owner is unaware that a manager gave such a lease or that the tenant has fabricated or altered the actual valid lease. Or it could be that the owner is so desperate to sell that the owner has "invented" the lease.

An estoppel letter, signed by every tenant will protect you against such episodes. This letter spells out the terms of a lease or has attached to it a copy of the lease, and both the owner of the building and the tenant sign it, attesting that the terms contained in the attached document (or in the letter) are the true and only terms and conditions of the lease.

Overly Friendly Leases

Short and sweet—but too much so—leases might be okay, but they can lead to big problems, especially if you want to sell the building. I have seen many such leases, often executed by well intending people on both sides of the lease. Then times change, and the owner begins to have a problem with one or more of the tenants. The tenants get together, and one of them takes their lease to a lawyer, who realizes that the lease has more holes in the document than a sieve.

There are form leases that generally conform to the state landlord/tenant laws, which you can use if you do not want to use a lawyer's prepared lease. But take my advice, invest in a lawyer who will give you a lease that protects you.

Cutting Down on Maintenance

Most tenants respect a landlord's pride of ownership and will respond accordingly. When the building owner starts to cut down on maintenance, the reaction from the tenants can be negative. If there is going to be curtailing of some normally scheduled maintenance for a good reason, such as resurfacing the parking lot in three months and painting the building after that, a notice to the tenants might be advisable telling them that the usual cleaning around the building will be postponed until after the work is done.

However, regularly scheduled general maintenance is important and should be maintained on its normal schedule.

Under Insured

The day after you have reduced your casualty insurance or increased your deduction from $5,000 to $15,000 is the day the storm hits. Protect your assets, and your bank account, by maintaining a good level of insurance. Weigh the difference in annual premium between the $5,000 deductible and that of $15,000. If the few hundred dollars you save means so much to you, then what about the extra $10,000, you may have to pay to cover the damage.

Shop around for insurance, but make sure that you know what coverage you are getting. You might think that the two policies (offered to you by two different companies) are the same except for the premium, but when carefully read, and compared by every coverage and condition, you might discover that the one that is $2,000 cheaper has some holes in the coverage that make it far less attractive.

Management by Default

Management by default is when you do nothing to resolve a pending problem or condition. This is often the case with absentee management, where there is little or no hands on attention by the owner or professional property manager. Good property management demands that someone regularly visit the property. Contact with the tenants should include periodic person-to-person conversations about how things are going. Is everything working, are there leaks, are there any problems that need attention? This kind of management lets the tenants know that you or the management team is on top of the situation, and problems do not generally occur or when they do they are minor and can be quickly dealt with.

Code Violations

City code violations may go undetected for years. They are often the result of something tenants have done to their leased space. Management or the property owner may also be unaware of the problem because there has not been any detailed inspections of the property for a long period of time, perhaps never during the tenant's tenure. Then the lease is up, and no renewal is made. That tenant leaves, and the management or property owner has a painter go in and clean out the space, put a fresh coat of paint and install the FOR RENT sign.

Along comes a new tenant who signs a lease and in the process of moving in has a city occupational license inspection. Now we learn that there is a major code violation in the way in which the back area of the space has been remodeled. Plumbing has been rearranged, walls moved, or torn down—all without a permit.

These situations can be costly and very time consuming. To avoid them, make sure that inspections of the premises are frequent and that one last inspection before the tenant moves out is undertaken. All leases should have provisions that no changes in the premises can be made without the owner's approval and that all work approved must be done by licensed contractors with a valid building permit. Any work not so undertaken will be a violation of the lease and the tenant will responsible for repair or replacement of the premises in its prior condition and for any city code violations and penalties assessed.

Start Opening Doors Today

You plan for success begins now. Cash flow or equity buildup is moot unless you have made a sound investment. The objective you should have in sight before you acquire any real estate is to acquire a property that has the potential for both. How you structure the deal will shape which element you have prioritized. The ability for a property to eventually produce more revenue than expenses is critical to the overall process. Some investments will be alligators and eat your capital. Vacant land does this, and so will an economic conversion that is in the middle of becoming something new. But in the end, a successful investment is the one that brings you cash, either in monthly rent, or at the end of the day when you sell it.

The doors that you open will generally be there without anyone knocking from the other side. What is on the other side is opportunity. Contrary to the old saying that "opportunity only knocks once," it rarely knocks at all. Your opportunities are there, waiting for you to recognize then. It is up to you to learn where they are.

Constant Mortgage Rates
12 Monthly Payments a Year

Interest Years	5½%	5¾%	6%	6¼%	6½%	6¾%	7%	7¼%	7½%	7¾%
0.5	203.26	203.38	203.55	203.67	203.84	203.96	204.13	204.26	204.42	204.55
1.0	103.02	103.15	103.30	103.42	103.57	103.70	103.84	103.97	104.12	104.25
1.5	69.62	69.75	69.89	70.02	70.16	70.29	70.43	70.56	70.70	70.83
2.0	52.92	53.05	53.19	53.32	53.46	53.59	53.73	53.86	54.00	54.14
2.5	42.91	43.04	43.18	43.31	43.45	43.58	43.72	43.86	44.00	44.13
3.0	36.24	36.37	36.51	36.64	36.78	36.92	37.06	37.19	37.33	37.47
3.5	31.48	31.61	31.75	31.89	32.03	32.16	32.30	32.44	32.58	32.71
4.0	27.91	28.05	28.19	28.32	28.46	28.60	28.74	28.88	29.02	29.16
4.5	25.14	25.28	25.42	25.55	25.69	25.83	25.97	26.11	26.25	26.39
5.0	22.93	23.06	23.20	23.34	23.48	23.62	23.76	23.90	24.05	24.19
5.5	21.12	21.25	21.39	21.53	21.68	21.82	21.96	22.10	22.25	22.39
6.0	19.61	19.75	19.89	20.03	20.17	20.32	20.46	20.60	20.75	20.89
6.5	18.34	18.48	18.62	18.76	18.91	19.05	19.19	19.34	19.49	19.63
7.0	17.25	17.39	17.53	17.68	17.82	17.97	18.11	18.26	18.41	18.55
7.5	16.30	16.45	16.59	16.74	16.88	17.03	17.18	17.32	17.47	17.62
8.0	15.48	15.63	15.77	15.92	16.07	16.21	16.36	16.51	16.66	16.81
8.5	14.76	14.90	15.05	15.20	15.35	15.49	15.64	15.79	15.95	16.10
9.0	14.11	14.26	14.41	14.56	14.71	14.86	15.01	15.16	15.31	15.47
9.5	13.54	13.69	13.84	13.99	14.14	14.29	14.44	14.59	14.75	14.91
10.0	13.03	13.17	13.32	13.47	13.63	13.78	13.93	14.09	14.25	14.40
10.5	12.56	12.71	12.86	13.01	13.17	13.32	13.48	13.63	13.79	13.95
11.0	12.14	12.29	12.44	12.59	12.75	12.90	13.06	13.22	13.38	13.54
11.5	11.75	11.91	12.06	12.21	12.37	12.53	12.69	12.84	13.00	13.17
12.0	11.40	11.56	11.71	11.87	12.02	12.18	12.34	12.50	12.66	12.83
12.5	11.08	11.24	11.39	11.55	11.71	11.87	12.03	12.19	12.35	12.52
13.0	10.79	10.96	11.10	11.26	11.42	11.58	11.74	11.90	12.07	12.23
13.5	10.51	10.67	10.83	10.90	11.15	11.31	11.47	11.64	11.80	11.97
14.0	10.26	10.42	10.58	10.74	10.90	11.06	11.23	11.39	11.56	11.73
14.5	10.02	10.18	10.34	10.50	10.67	10.83	11.00	11.16	11.33	11.50
15.0	9.81	9.97	10.13	10.29	10.45	10.62	10.79	10.95	11.12	11.30
15.5	9.60	9.76	9.93	10.09	10.26	10.42	10.59	10.76	10.93	11.10
16.0	9.41	9.57	9.74	9.90	10.07	10.24	10.41	10.58	10.75	10.92
16.5	9.24	9.40	9.56	9.73	9.90	10.07	10.24	10.41	10.58	10.76
17.0	9.07	9.23	9.40	9.56	9.73	9.90	10.08	10.25	10.42	10.60
17.5	8.91	9.08	9.24	9.41	9.58	9.75	9.93	10.10	10.28	10.46
18.0	8.76	8.93	9.10	9.27	9.44	9.61	9.79	9.96	10.14	10.32
18.5	8.63	8.79	8.96	9.13	9.31	9.48	9.65	9.83	10.01	10.19
19.0	8.50	8.66	8.83	9.01	9.18	9.35	9.53	9.71	9.89	10.07
19.5	8.37	8.54	8.71	8.88	9.06	9.24	9.41	9.59	9.78	9.96
20.0	8.26	8.43	8.60	8.77	8.95	9.12	9.30	9.48	9.67	9.85
20.5	8.15	8.32	8.49	8.66	8.84	9.02	9.20	9.38	9.57	9.75
21.0	8.04	8.21	8.39	8.56	8.74	8.92	9.10	9.29	9.47	9.66
21.5	7.94	8.11	8.29	8.47	8.65	8.83	9.01	9.19	9.38	9.57
22.0	7.85	8.02	8.20	8.38	8.56	8.74	8.92	9.11	9.29	9.48
22.5	7.76	7.93	8.11	8.29	8.47	8.65	8.84	9.02	9.21	9.40
23.0	7.67	7.85	8.03	8.21	8.39	8.57	8.76	8.95	9.14	9.33
23.5	7.59	7.77	7.95	8.13	8.31	8.50	8.68	8.87	9.06	9.26
24.0	7.51	7.69	7.87	9.05	8.24	8.42	8.61	8.80	9.00	9.19
24.5	7.44	7.62	7.80	7.98	8.17	8.36	8.55	8.74	8.93	9.12
25.0	7.37	7.55	7.73	7.92	8.10	8.29	8.48	8.67	8.87	9.06
25.5	7.30	7.48	7.67	7.85	8.04	8.23	8.42	8.61	8.81	9.01
26.0	7.24	7.42	7.60	7.79	7.98	8.17	8.36	8.56	8.75	8.95
26.5	7.18	7.36	7.55	7.73	7.92	8.11	8.31	8.50	8.70	8.90
27.0	7.12	7.30	7.49	7.68	7.87	8.06	8.25	8.45	8.65	8.85
27.5	7.06	7.25	7.43	7.62	7.81	8.01	8.20	8.40	8.60	8.80
28.0	7.01	7.19	7.38	7.57	7.76	7.96	8.16	8.35	8.55	8.76
28.5	6.96	7.14	7.33	7.52	7.72	7.91	8.11	8.31	9.51	8.71
29.0	6.91	7.09	7.28	7.48	7.67	7.87	8.07	8.27	8.47	8.67
29.5	6.86	7.05	7.24	7.43	7.63	7.82	8.02	8.23	8.43	8.63
30.0	6.81	7.00	7.20	7.39	7.59	7.78	7.98	8.19	8.39	8.60
35.0	6.44	6.64	6.84	7.05	7.25	7.46	7.67	7.88	8.09	8.31

Constant Mortgage Rates 12 Monthly Payments a Year

8%	8¼%	8½%	8¾%	9%	9¼%	9½%	9¾%	10%	11%	12%
204.71	204.87	205.00	205.16	205.29	205.45	205.58	205.74	205.88	206.49	207.07
104.39	104.54	104.67	104.81	104.95	105.09	105.22	105.37	105.50	106.07	106.63
70.97	71.11	71.25	71.39	71.52	71.66	71.79	71.94	72.07	72.63	73.18
54.28	54.42	54.55	54.69	54.82	54.96	55.10	55.24	55.37	55.93	56.49
44.27	44.41	44.54	44.68	44.82	44.96	45.10	25.24	45.37	45.94	46.50
37.61	37.75	37.88	38.02	38.16	38.30	38.44	38.58	38.72	39.29	39.86
32.85	33.00	33.13	33.28	33.41	33.56	33.70	33.84	33.98	34.56	35.13
29.30	29.44	29.58	29.72	29.86	30.01	30.15	30.29	30.44	31.02	31.60
26.54	26.68	26.82	26.97	27.11	27.25	27.40	27.54	27.69	28.28	28.87
24.33	24.48	24.62	24.77	24.91	25.06	25.20	25.35	25.50	26.09	26.69
22.54	22.68	22.83	22.97	23.12	23.27	23.41	23.56	23.71	24.32	24.93
21.04	21.19	21.33	21.48	21.63	21.78	21.93	22.06	22.23	22.84	23.46
19.78	19.93	20.08	20.23	20.38	20.53	20.68	20.83	20.98	21.60	22.23
18.70	18.86	19.00	19.16	19.31	19.46	19.61	19.77	19.92	20.55	21.18
17.77	17.93	18.08	18.23	18.38	18.54	18.69	18.85	19.01	19.64	20.28
16.96	17.12	17.27	17.43	17.58	17.74	17.89	18.05	18.21	18.85	19.50
16.25	16.41	16.56	16.72	16.88	17.03	17.19	17.35	17.51	18.16	18.82
15.62	15.78	15.94	16.09	16.25	16.41	16.57	16.73	16.89	17.55	18.22
15.06	15.22	15.38	15.54	15.70	15.86	16.02	16.18	16.35	17.01	17.69
14.56	14.72	14.88	15.04	15.20	15.36	15.53	15.69	15.86	16.53	17.22
14.11	14.27	14.43	14.59	14.76	14.92	15.09	15.25	15.42	16.10	16.79
13.70	13.86	14.02	14.19	14.35	14.52	14.69	14.86	15.02	15.71	16.41
13.33	13.49	13.66	13.82	13.99	14.16	14.33	14.50	14.67	15.36	16.07
12.99	13.16	13.32	13.49	13.66	13.83	14.00	14.17	14.34	15.04	15.76
12.68	12.85	13.02	13.18	13.35	13.53	13.70	13.87	14.04	14.75	15.48
12.40	12.57	12.73	12.91	13.08	13.25	13.42	13.60	13.77	14.49	15.22
12.14	12.31	12.48	12.65	12.82	13.00	13.17	13.35	13.53	14.25	14.99
11.90	12.07	12.24	12.41	12.59	12.76	12.94	13.12	13.30	14.03	14.78
11.67	11.85	12.02	12.20	12.37	12.55	12.73	12.91	13.09	13.83	14.58
11.47	11.64	11.82	11.99	12.17	12.35	12.53	12.71	12.90	13.64	14.40
11.28	11.45	11.63	11.81	11.99	12.17	12.35	12.53	12.72	13.47	14.24
11.10	11.28	11.45	11.63	11.81	12.00	12.18	12.37	12.55	13.31	14.09
10.93	11.11	11.29	11.47	11.65	11.84	12.02	12.21	12.40	13.16	13.94
10.78	10.96	11.14	11.32	11.51	11.69	11.88	12.07	12.25	13.03	13.81
10.64	10.82	11.00	11.18	11.37	11.55	11.74	11.93	12.12	12.90	13.69
10.50	10.68	10.87	11.05	11.24	11.43	11.62	11.61	12.00	12.78	13.58
10.37	10.56	10.74	10.93	11.12	11.31	11.50	11.69	11.88	12.67	13.48
10.25	10.44	10.63	10.81	11.00	11.19	11.39	11.58	11.78	12.57	13.38
10.14	10.33	10.52	10.71	10.90	11.09	11.28	11.48	11.67	12.48	13.30
10.04	10.23	10.41	10.60	10.80	10.99	11.19	11.38	11.58	12.39	13.21
9.94	10.13	10.32	10.51	10.70	10.90	11.09	11.29	11.49	12.30	13.14
9.85	10.04	10.23	10.42	10.62	10.81	11.01	11.21	11.41	12.23	13.06
9.76	9.95	10.14	10.34	10.53	10.73	10.93	11.13	11.33	12.15	13.00
9.67	9.87	10.06	10.26	10.45	10.65	10.85	11.06	11.26	12.09	12.94
9.60	9.79	9.99	10.18	10.38	10.58	10.78	10.99	11.19	12.02	12.88
9.52	9.72	9.91	10.11	10.31	10.51	10.72	10.92	11.13	11.96	12.82
9.45	9.65	9.85	10.05	10.25	10.45	10.65	10.86	11.07	11.91	12.77
9.38	9.58	9.78	9.98	10.18	10.39	10.59	10.80	11.01	11.86	12.72
9.32	9.52	9.72	9.92	10.13	10.33	10.54	10.75	10.96	11.81	12.68
9.26	9.46	9.66	9.87	10.07	10.28	10.48	10.69	10.90	11.76	12.64
9.21	9.41	9.61	9.81	10.02	10.23	10.43	10.65	10.86	11.72	12.60
9.15	9.35	9.56	9.76	9.97	10.18	10.39	10.60	10.81	11.68	12.56
9.10	9.30	9.51	9.71	9.92	10.13	10.34	10.56	10.77	11.64	12.53
9.05	9.26	9.46	9.67	9.88	10.09	10.30	10.51	10.73	11.60	12.50
9.01	9.21	9.42	9.63	9.84	10.05	10.26	10.48	10.69	11.57	12.47
8.96	9.17	9.38	9.58	9.80	10.01	10.22	10.44	10.66	11.54	12.44
8.92	9.13	9.34	9.55	9.76	9.97	10.19	10.40	10.62	11.51	12.41
8.88	9.09	9.30	9.51	9.72	9.94	10.15	10.37	10.59	11.48	12.39
8.84	9.05	9.26	9.47	9.69	9.90	10.12	10.34	10.56	11.45	12.37
8.81	9.02	9.23	9.44	9.66	9.87	10.09	10.31	10.53	11.43	12.34
8.52	8.74	8.96	9.18	9.41	9.63	9.86	10.09	10.32	11.24	12.19